Executive Speech Doctor

Executive Speech Doctor

*Engaging with Community
Audiences in Person and Online*

ROBERT J. WEIS

Foreword by Randy C. James

McFarland & Company, Inc., Publishers
Jefferson, North Carolina

LIBRARY OF CONGRESS CATALOGUING-IN-PUBLICATION DATA

Names: Weis, Robert J., author. | James, Randy C., writer of foreword.
Title: Executive speech doctor : engaging with community audiences in person and online / Robert J. Weis ; foreword by Randy C. James.
Description: Jefferson, North Carolina : McFarland & Company, Inc., Publishers, 2023 | Includes bibliographical references and index.
Identifiers: LCCN 2023008790 | ISBN 9781476691664 (paperback : acid free paper) ∞ \ISBN 9781476648965 (ebook)
Subjects: LCSH: Public speaking. | Business communication.
Classification: LCC PN4193.B8 W45 2023 | DDC 808.5/1—dc23/eng/20230412
LC record available at https://lccn.loc.gov/2023008790

BRITISH LIBRARY CATALOGUING DATA ARE AVAILABLE

ISBN (print) 978-1-4766-9166-4
ISBN (ebook) 978-1-4766-4896-5

Front cover images © cupuuu25/samui/Shutterstock

Printed in the United States of America

McFarland & Company, Inc., Publishers
Box 611, Jefferson, North Carolina 28640
www.mcfarlandpub.com

To my parents, my loving wife, and my family

Table of Contents

Acknowledgments

This book stems from a variety of experiences, sources, encouragement, and reviews of draft material. Accomplished author and longtime friend Vic Kucera sparked my interest in writing a book like this. He discussed ideas with me, reviewed drafts of chapters and encouraged me all along the way. For this I am especially grateful.

I thank my advisor in Ph.D. studies in Communications at the University of Washington, Keith R. Stamm, now professor emeritus, who initially supported my development of "questioning tactics" as my advisor for my dissertation research. Another member of my doctoral committee, Richard F. Carter, professor emeritus and lifetime achievement award-winner from fellow communication theorists, has continued to be a wellspring for my work all along.

In reading my draft materials, Prof. Stamm confirmed my use of research on "community ties" including studies that we conducted together and affirmed my use of classic literature on "co-orientation" theory. As a key developer of co-orientation research to begin with, he endorsed my formulation in this book of the overall concept of "co-questioning" and its components. He also encouraged my persistence in further theory construction and formulating the concept of "empathetic outreach," and my focus on combining this with co-questioning to establish an unprecedented seven-step model for executive public speaking to community audiences.

In writing this book it was heartwarming to look back through my records, pull together memories, and collect examples and stories related to a wide variety of employers, top executives, and clients. If this seems exuberant, you would understand readily if you knew these stellar leaders in business, profit and not-for-profit, at the local, national, and international levels.

Major interviewees who added depth of insight and practical experience on topics ranging from the dynamics of giving online talks to what program and conference chairs look for and to the dynamics of serving on a panel include Phyllis Campbell, Diane Douglas, Ted Leonhardt, Mike Olden, and Hayden Williams.

Looking back, my experiences in public speech outreach planning, research (including market research) and extensive writing, training and rehearsing, and evaluation tracking all seem to have a pleasing coherence at this point. I hope this is evident in the construction of this book as well. Along the road, however, the way wasn't always so certain and smooth, given corporate restructuring, the Great Recession, executive reassignments, retirements and finding new clients, changes in technology, and ups and downs in the business cycle.

Key individuals who have been a positive influence along the way include the following who kindly reviewed a draft of the book for the sake of writing a foreword or endorsements: Randy C. James, Luke Helms, Kim Mackay, Art Merrick, and Ted Leonhardt. Their suggestions and thoughts are most appreciated.

Fellow graduate students at the University of Washington, who by now are professors emeriti or engaged in community service, have supported me at least in spirit for many years. Particularly valuable for this book have been the research and publications developed by esteemed colleague and faithful friend Hak-Soo Kim of Sogang University in South Korea. His works on community problem-solving and co-communicating are classic.

Professional sources who have helped me with technical points in developing this book include Daniel Berg, Bridget Weis, James P. Murphy, Frank R. Weis, and Peter S. Wong.

Finally, yet most important, I give due credit and my love and affection to my wife and children, who are ever inspiring, wise, and kind.

Foreword

by Randy C. James

Robert Weis is unique in the world of speech science. He has captured the transitional essence of how giving speeches in a dynamic world has changed over the years.

When I graduated summa cum laude in Speech Communications from the University of Washington years ago, I thought I was ready to conquer the world. I took my new degree and went directly into teaching speech at the high school and college levels. During those teaching days I learned a valuable lesson. Greek scholars, as Dr. Weis points out, such as Socrates, Plato, and Aristotle, were taught to me as the greatest orators of all time. I immediately started training students in the "Art of Persuasion" that these Greek orators were so famous for creating and that found their way into the college courses across America. However, this book will show you the problem with that approach.

Dr. Weis, whom I have known for years, is a disciplined teacher and great observer. He watched executives, like me, struggle through the rigors of making speeches to a variety of audiences. He stepped in as the "CEO Speech Doctor" and began to reshape how executives and community leaders presented their material to a variety of audiences. He has transitioned us in his counseling to the relational role of co-questioning and empathetic outreach public speaking.

For many years I've worked diligently to follow the principles Dr. Weis fosters. In preparing to speak to a broad base of banking clients, community organizations, U.S. Senate briefings, and even large teacher groups, I've made use of his principles for listening to the needs of the audience prior to creating my speeches. In this book Dr. Weis lays out the critical elements for how to do the advance research about your audiences to be certain your speech addresses the subject from the perspective of their thoughts and feelings.

In my early days of college training, I was taught to develop a speaking

1

outline, even the structure of three key points as Dr. Weis teaches in this book. He, however, shows you the exact procedure necessary to make your outline fit your audience and how to tailor it to the time allotted for maximum effectiveness. The book also gives important ways to address a Question-and-Answer phase at the conclusion of your prepared remarks.

Finally, as we all know, the platform for speaking events has dramatically changed over the years. This change has left many key speakers hungry for ways to adapt. For speaking at breakfast, lunch, or even dinner meetings of community leaders, speakers now may be presenting their speech material online from a desktop in their own home. This has seen many well-known executives refrain from even trying to adapt to these new conditions. Dr. Weis has this covered.

In this book you will learn not only how to prepare your material, but also how to present it either in-person or in accord with online fundamentals. From discussing lighting and camera angles to even whether to sit or stand while speaking, his helpful tips show us how to deal readily with today's technological world and keep up with new developments.

Too many times, as an executive attending speaking events, I have been dismayed at how poorly speakers prepare, how poorly they present, and how disconnected they are from the interests and needs of the audience. This book will fix that if you're willing to engage and practice what Dr. Weis presents. Be "relational," and enjoy your opportunities.

Randy C. James has served as a Pacific Northwest bank CEO, corporate director, community leader, teacher, author, and independent financial consultant.

Preface

If you are or aspire to be a top executive, make the most of your opportunities to reach out and speak to community forums on behalf of your team. To help resolve divisiveness and to strengthen mutual respect and cooperation, let's consider how leaders like you can engage skillfully with public audiences in-person and virtually.

This book offers new insights and proven guidance for connecting with public audiences with insight, respect, and positive results. This pointed advice is based on graduate education and communication science and on extensive practical experience on the job and in the community. After studies in philosophy (B.A., Mt. Angel Seminary College in Oregon) and theology (University of Innsbruck, Austria), I graduated with an M.A. in journalism/public relations from the University of Oregon. I also was an honor graduate of the Defense Information school at Ft. Benjamin Harrison, Indiana, and served in the U.S. Army Reserve with duties including editing a regional Army news publication.

My professional experience includes work in corporate public relations in Portland, Oregon, and Seattle, Washington, at what today is part of the telecommunications firm Lumen. My responsibilities ranged from media relations and employee and management communications, to serving as staff manager of a corporate slide-production unit. Later, after earning my Ph.D. from the University of Washington in Seattle, with emphasis on communication theory and research methodology as well as community development, my further corporate PR experience included "issues management" and corporate executive speech management, and speechwriting in Seattle for what's now part of Bank of America.

Thereafter I took that bank work out on contract and developed new clients as an independent consultant, serving as "Weis Communications" for many years. My consulting work applied lessons learned in executive speech management and writing to support more than 40 top executives in enterprises large and small, speaking at the regional, national, and international levels. After retiring in 2019 I began work on this book, including developing the scientific concepts of co-questioning and empathetic outreach, envisioning them in a combination reaction.

The net result of this scholarly research and professional experience is a new approach to:

- Identifying listeners' interests and concerns,
- Developing responsive speech material that works,
- Delivering with confidence,
- Earning respect,
- Supporting your team,
- Achieving your personal goals,
- Making a positive difference in the community.

The guidelines that follow apply whether you lead an innovative start-up, a hard-charging small or medium-sized business, a service-minded not-for-profit, a professional firm, a multi-state retailer, or are the head of an employee or a civil service organization, or work in public education, an international corporation, or a biomedical or technology superstar.

The time for such outreach in the community is now. For most any business today and in the days ahead, the challenges are complex if not daunting. Distrust of social institutions in general has risen.[1] Public audiences in communities you serve wonder if business leaders like you understand—or even care—what the general public worries about, wants and expects.

Through your public speaking you can listen to and identify public expectations and hopes, share mutual concerns and values, and open new doors for customers, your team, and your future.

Accordingly, this book steps up with 45 chapters of guidance for effective speaking to audiences in communities you serve. Some chapters are brief, some longer, all written in executive-summary style. You'll find recommendations—tested, tried, and true—to help you zero in with a strategic approach to getting invited to speak to community audiences, as well as values, principles, and mechanics you can apply in researching, writing, and polishing your remarks.

You'll see that your first step toward skillful public-speaking is a matter of insight: a successful public speech is not so much about you, it's relational. It's much more about listening in advance to key members of your audience, getting a good sense of how they are thinking and feeling about topics you intend to address, and then responding with seasoned effectiveness.

Fundamentals

CHAPTER 1

Co-Questioning
and Empathetic Outreach

Although you may see this book's approach to public speaking as common sense, it's something totally new, a breakthrough that can change the world of executive public speaking. One top communication scientist termed this as "revolutionary" … "a new paradigm."[1]

The new paradigm is the following combination of key elements:

- An emphasis on outreach to listen to relevant interests, thoughts, preconceptions, and feelings of your audience before developing the text of a speech you plan to give.
- A mutual spirit of inquiry, interest and analysis—co-questioning[2]—as you address your topic in a way that takes into account your listeners' way of thinking and is open to their responses and questions.
- A broad pattern of "questioning tactics" that can help you identify patterns of thought the audience may have in mind about you and your topic and that you can use to develop your main points supporting the overall theme of your remarks.
- A new focus on executive "empathetic outreach," a new concept for taking into account audience emotions related to topics you choose to cover.
- An overall intent to develop a relationship with audience members as you respond to their interests, introduce your views, clarify your points, and open new doors for mutual benefit.
- Appreciating what you learn from your audience: questions, ideas, complaints, suggestions, observations, requests for new products or services, and thought-starters you can develop further in your community outreach and in the office.

Traditional Approach

By contrast, consider the traditional approach to community outreach public speaking, still practiced today by too many executives, often as advised by professionals in public and community relations—including some professional speechwriters:

- Wanting to speak to the public in order to express "messages" about new priorities.
- Focusing on the executive's and the company's vision and strengths, including new products and services.
- Getting maximum "impact" with a script that is smooth and to the point in expressing what you want to say.
- Delivering the message with good dynamics, emphasis, and energy, perhaps with the help of a speech coach in order to make a better "impression."
- Being able to handle any difficult questions at the end by getting "media training" on how to handle media-type questions, particularly how to "bounce back" from any invasive and difficult questions like what a news reporter might ask.
- Above all, being persuasive, dynamic, hitting your "target" spot-on.

At first this may sound very good; there's nothing totally misguided about all of this—but this approach is all about you, the speaker. Instead, your focus should be on the audience—particularly at the outset. Puzzling? Let's think this through.

Beyond Persuasion

Traditionally, speech training and development for centuries has nestled comfortably in the familiar—but dysfunctional—perspective of "persuasion." This traditional model of public speaking traces back at least to the rhetoric of ancient Greeks speaking in law courts to win cases for their clients, and through the years especially characterizes political speeches of all kinds.

Persuasion still today has its relevance for attorneys, debaters, advertisers, and other advocates. In general, we still hear speech advice to "tell them what you want to tell them, then tell them (in detail), and finally tell them what you told them." Attractive at first, powerful, righteous. But it's top-down, essentially arrogant, and it can be off-putting—particularly for audiences today who are on the alert about being bullied by authoritarian figures.

Relational

The new co-questioning model this book advocates focuses on being relational, connecting with the audience in ways sensitive to their perspectives. This includes an emphasis on taking an approach that builds on their point of view, considers sharing thoughts, interests and sentiments, and develops your ideas in ways that make sense to them. In fact, this co-questioning approach could serve as a general model for professional community relations if not public relations in general.

An efficient way to begin listening to a speech audience is to interview in advance two or three carefully-selected members of that audience, exploring how they feel about the whole idea of your speech, their ways of thinking about your topic, interests that you should address. This can include their predispositions, and specific questions that could come up. In making such contacts—in market research termed "key person interviews"—you also may pick up latent emotions about your topic, get a sense of their candid impressions and their experiences with your industry in general if not your enterprise, and be reminded of useful stories you could tell and audience members likely would appreciate.

In paying special attention to the audience in advance, although you may find there may be negatives in the picture, you'll likely see new grounds for interests you have in common and for creating mutual understanding. You may find your audience would want to hear more about special values mutually important to them and to you, and about specific new developments in your industry.

A key point is that in talking about your industry in general, you're not directly "selling" your enterprise, but you're opening the door for good outcomes you are focusing on as top priorities.

So the point is to help your listeners think with you about new and promising initiatives, values you hold in common, and why they can feel good about supporting you and your associates—as customers, investors, and co-members of the community.

Technically, this approach stems from an earlier paradigm shift in communication science called "co-orientation," rooted originally in consideration of two individuals' relating to an object of interest in a balanced way.[3] This led to concern with matching ways of thinking,[4] and later to communication researchers Chaffee and McLeod's general co-orientation model,[5] broadly considered, often applied with implications for professional public relations.[6] Working from that model, communication scientists Stamm and Pearce took a major step forward in a co-orientation experiment finding that "congruency" with an audience—whether their views are similar to one's own to begin with—tends to be especially important in interpersonal communication.[7] As Stamm later observed, "When expected congruency turns out to be inaccurate, lots of questioning behavior is produced as a result. Imagine a speaker who wrongly assumes that the members of an audience will agree with what the speaker is about to say, and then is confronted with a torrent of questions the speaker did not anticipate."[8]

For us, the importance of this finding is that if we first stop, listen in advance and take into consideration the thoughts that characterize our audience, then we can be more successful in constructing and conveying the main theme and key points of a speech effectively.

In this book, the overall co-questioning model for public speaking goes on to include classic speech structure and dynamics, and observations from this author's depth of experience as a corporate speech manager and independent speech strategist, researcher and writer working with a diversity of business and not-for-profit executives in enterprises large and small.

For you this new model sets up patterns that help make your outreach to community audiences especially productive and worthwhile—for everyone concerned.

CHAPTER 2

Virtual vs. In-Person Public Speaking

We've come a long way since the introduction of the "Virtual Era"[1] just a short time ago. As one colleague puts it, "Everyone in business is doing video, Zoom, Google, Teams, and such several times a day. It's as assumed and familiar as a phone conversation was in the past."[2]

Although you may not be looking for training to handle virtual connections, when it comes to public speaking to a community audience, there are some key differences—opportunities and pitfalls to be aware of. Speaking to a community audience that you don't know personally is quite different from just making a call. Let's take a closer look.

Getting Ready for a Virtual Speech

If you are invited to speak at a public online forum, such as a large service club or a civic club, a chamber of commerce, a professional association, or an industry conference, connect with the group's production staff as soon as possible to begin to make arrangements, to learn production tech requirements, and to set a date for a trial run.

If you do it yourself, speaking to perhaps a smaller forum from your own premises as the host, be sure your hardware and software are reasonably up to date. Consider the following levels of tech in the order of "professionalism" most people would consider:

- Basic: Laptop or tablet on a stand for a forehead level camera angle (higher than eyes is better for the most attractive camera angle).
- One step up: Upgrade to a webcam with built-in noise cancelling microphone and auto-adjustment for dim lighting.
- Next step up: Add a single ring light above and behind the webcam setup for even, full-face lighting.

- Most advanced (more commonly for professional recording, such as podcasting): Add a USB condenser microphone for ultra-crisp audio.

If you're using a specialized camera, place it over a monitor so you easily can "read" the audience on the monitor as you speak. Yet make sure to keep maximum eye contact with the camera—your audience—as you speak. In addition, arrange your notes adjacent to the participant view, both just underneath your camera so that you are able to look at it all together.

Host or Guest Speaker?

If you'll be online as a guest speaker interacting with a host, you'll need to get in sync by meeting with the host online in advance and thinking through, perhaps outlining, how you will collaborate on-screen. You'll likely need to meet with the host one-on-one to see how the host interacts.

If you'll be the host yourself, get an experienced coach to help you master the use of basic Zoom-type controls including "muting" participants and admitting participants from a "waiting room"—which works differently depending on the video calling platform in use. Another important control is "spotlighting," which is how to make someone the point of focus for the whole list of attendees. As a presenter you also should decide how calling controls like "hand-raise" and "chat" will come into play; decide how to give the audience those directions at the start.

You'll also need to learn to handle screen-sharing to be able to show slides (PowerPoint, for example) efficiently, with confidence.

In any case, practice speaking to the camera, not to the "gallery"— this takes concentrated effort because it's so easy to end up speaking to those images rather than to the eye of a camera. When you do not speak to the camera, you lose eye contact with your audience!

Looking Good

For a good image on-camera be sure your face is well lit, with very little backlighting (which darkens your image). It helps to have the camera (or your computer camera) slightly above eye-level, at forehead or hairline level, to prevent flattening your face. In addition, remember that you are composing a complete picture, so check your on-screen background.

Watch and learn from your peers what works well in the background materials they set up and use. You even could look for virtual backgrounds online, but don't get carried away with that. In many cases there is a special background that the speaker should use for the event or the topic, rather than a standard background. Be careful about what items appear in the background. It's best to keep your background relatively simple, and in good taste.

Being Good

For a major executive speech rather than just an online meeting or chat session, if you are able, make use of the services of a speech professional (speechwriter, delivery coach, or both). Prepare, don't "wing it." In this author's experience, for a top-level corporate executive it can be critical to get professional support from the start to ensure continuity, well-researched material, staying on schedule, and getting useful feedback.

Make sure you and the writer meet with the production team early in the process—the sooner the better.

It always pays to set up a production schedule, including arrangements for a trial run, and for testing the equipment, and seeing how your production will look on video. If you will be working with a host and technical team at a major public forum, make sure your team gets in touch with them early. Appoint someone to keep everyone involved on schedule and in sync.

CHAPTER 3

Proficient Virtual Delivery

As you set out to give speeches online, start with smaller, less formal groups who would be more forgiving if you're not a virtual superstar. To be strategic and to improve your delivery skills on-camera, make a plan to give such speeches on a regular basis. Move up to more challenging forums as you go, paying attention to feedback, and getting professional guidance if possible as you go in order to improve your use of technology and your interaction skills. With reasonable effort, you'll be more effective than most executives trying to use new technology.

In any event, on the day of a talk, be sure to have tech help standing by in case there are equipment problems. Be ready to handle trouble if any, so that when you speak you can concentrate on your audience and what you have to say, and—above all—not waste your audience's time.

Learn from Feedback

After your virtual speech, get some feedback from peers, associates, and friends about how you look on-screen, about the overall setup, about how you come across, your chemistry with the audience, the way you handle questions—and especially about what you said or didn't say. You could do this yourself, but it helps to have a third party—especially a pro who knows what to look for and ask about—get such feedback for you.

As technology advances and offers more capabilities, online equipment will become more complex, yet could make it all easier to get everything in order to enhance the value of virtual public speaking to community audiences, for everyone involved.

Shorter Is Better

What's emerged so far as the protocol for the content and style of online speeches? First consider that in general audiences today are drawn more and more to simple, clear-cut talks that don't waste time (this is especially important among younger audiences, who are used to efficient video presentations on the job), no matter who's involved and how impressive the platform.

For many years the once-ubiquitous standard time frame for the often-termed "Iowa Rotary style of public speaking," typical for most community forums, was 20 minutes. In the world of tech videos today, the standard timing for still-popular TED (Technology, Entertainment, Design) Talks is 18 minutes. Today even podcasts are getting shorter.[1]

It may well be that 15- to 16-minute talks will become the new standard format for online community venues with small audiences, to allow more time for further online interaction and questions.

On the other hand, audiences tend to stick with an engaging speaker. If you find a 20-minute speech is still the norm for your audience, that can work to your benefit if you prepare accordingly.

Overall, identify the desired timing for the group you'll address so that you fit in with the perspective and style of engagement that works best for them.

Context

Know the context of your audience. If they will be coming to your session after a day of back-to-back video meetings, they will be less likely to engage in a longer talk without breaks or audience participation. One sign of this is when most of your audience has their cameras turned off.

It can be especially challenging to give a talk to a group without any audience cameras turned on, because there are no mechanisms for you to see how your audience is responding.

If you are hoping for more engagement, start with a warm-up question for folks to answer in the chat, or ask a few pointed questions for the audience to consider for joining the conversation. Also, feel free to ask participants to turn on their cameras at the start as part of your meeting "rules" for virtual hand-raising, asking questions, muting, and using the chat feature.

If you plan to play a video, know that bandwidth will have a massive impact on the quality for participants. It is a common practice to ask participants to turn off their cameras to improve video playback and quality on their end.

Even so, consider the difference between an executive speech to a public audience when personal engagement is at a premium, and a presentation which can be an "information dump" that is not at all engaging.

Your goal in addressing a public audience should be to develop at least the beginnings of a personal relationship rather than simply transferring information.

Structure

In general, how should you structure a virtual speech? Research with program chairs at major community forums suggests that the heart of the online talk should still be the structure of a theme and three-major points, something we'll consider in more depth in later chapters. In almost any speech, you'll find a three-point structure will stimulate a natural flow of thought whereby your audience stays with you and "finishes" your speech at the same time you do—not before.

Good Timing

Although there may be no rule, if the request for a virtual speech is 18 minutes plus questions and time for any further interaction, let's parse the time in terms of structure. First would come the introduction by the host (you should provide a short write-up in advance to help keep it brief). Then comes your part:

- Your Opening: 1 minute to engage with viewers
- Theme: 1 minute or less
- Three Major Points: 5 minutes for each; 15 minutes total
- Summary and Conclusion: 1 minute

Obviously, making such timing work requires discipline. In giving examples and telling stories, make sure they are not too long. Yet be prepared with some additional material to add further remarks if desired, especially toward the end of your talk if there's time.

Work well in advance with the host or your producer on what's required and what's possible for visuals in an online speech. Don't make your slides or videos too complicated. It's usually best to keep things simple. If you sense something could need further explanation, practice a candid summary so you can be quick about it, especially in a Question-and-Answer (Q&A) period at the end of your talk.

Be Careful and Considerate

It's important for maintaining audience focus that you not use a lot of text slides. If you repeatedly show key points in text on the screen, such redundancy is boring, and can feel insulting to your audience. For a community audience, don't try to give a typical TED Talk. Your viewers are not fellow employees, and likely are not slide-deck enthusiasts. A community speech should be much more personal, relational.

A Little More Time?

If you have more time available, such as 20 minutes plus questions, and if you have good material, use it! Your time budget could mean:

- Opening: 1 minute
- Theme: 1 minute or less
- Three Major Points: 5–6 minutes for each
- Summary and Conclusion: 1 minute

It doesn't take much additional content to expand the time. Just adding an example or a story to each of your three major points could suffice. You could introduce more visuals if you can do so efficiently, but be careful not to overdo it.

If this sharp focus on minutes seems ridiculous, don't kid yourself. Discipline works.

Be Engaging

For an online speech, in the opening make a special effort to engage with the host and the viewers from the get-go, to establish rapport. You may be able to include visuals. And an informal, personal touch helps get beyond the technical feel of it all.

In acknowledging members of your audience, perhaps do a "shout out," saying "hello" to a couple of individuals you know well. Take note of viewers with time-of-day differences if any, and be sure to greet audience members in distant locations. But get up to speed quickly.

Sit or Stand for Virtual Delivery?

Although for an in-person audience you almost always would stand, should you stand for an online, virtual speech? For a top executive, it's an important question. The answer: "It depends."

The program manager of a large citywide service club, a highly sought venue for national-level speakers, advised standing up "to project better."[2] A common observation among producers on the internet, and in this author's opinion is that whether to stand or be seated depends on the seriousness of the situation, the authority or importance of the speaker, or both.

For one on-going, medium-sized peer-level forum for CEOs of businesses with revenue of at least $1 million, the group's production manager said the visual format he prefers depends on technical logistics. "For a video capture that is mostly chest and up," he said, "the person should probably be seated so they can't move around. With the camera shot this 'tight,' it would be very distracting if they're moving left and right out of the frame."

He added that "if the video capture is more wide-angle [showing most of the body], then standing is almost always more inviting and engaging."

For an interview on-camera involving two or more people, he said, "It's almost always more inviting to have the interviewer and the interviewee be seated.... The speaker should not just look at the interviewer, but should be sure to look into the camera. Eye contact with the camera—with your audience—is crucial."[3]

If your message consists of counsel and advice, if the style of the online forum typically is quite informal, and if the number of participants is relatively small, the look and tone of a "seated chat" may be ideal. This could help enable opening up into a discussion if time allows. It's possible to have the participants break into "chat rooms" if the host (or you, if you're the host) is experienced enough to handle it, to have individuals interact and then come back to report to the overall group. Such an arrangement, however, typically would be beyond the scope, time constraints, and purposes of a typical Chief Executive Officer (CEO) speech.

Technical Glitches

Be prepared for anything to go wrong with the video or with the audio, or both—too often something does. At one point this author served as a corporate visual production manager when video technology was not as sophisticated, and had to deal with many kinks and mishaps, including total system failures. Unsettling, to say the least.

No excuses! When in doubt, if you are uneasy about the technology, be sure a tech is involved in the setup and is onsite with you on the day of an online speech to make things right. If you arrange such support, you'll never be sorry.

Rehearse

If the online speech is worth giving, then it's worth rehearsing in advance—more than once if possible. Plan for at least one full rehearsal, onsite if possible if the production originates at a host's studio, to make sure all the equipment works well, the overall setting is good, the background is unobtrusive, you are comfortable, you look good, any back-and-forth conversations can go smoothly, and your speech makes sense online.

An online speech can take more performance energy than one might expect, especially in timing the lead-in, progressing smoothly through main points, the use of slides and/or a video clip, comfortable interaction with audience members, and a finish with an earnest conclusion—on time. As you gain experience, it'll be much easier all around.

Remember that, above all, the virtual speech is meant to be quite "personal" for you and the audience. With enough practice in advance, and with experience, you'll make it easier to focus on the audience as you speak. Your goal should be to make your talk be as comfortable for everyone involved as if you were conversing with your friends.

Your Image On-Screen

Double-check the lighting on your face. It should be bright with no shadows; you may need to adjust the lighting to deal with this. Pay close attention to your appearance. Practice with the camera to make sure you look the way you'd like to present yourself to your audience.

In addition, your on-screen face should present your eyes at about one-third of the way down from the top of the frame—this is in accord with the classic design "rule of thirds." Keep in mind that you are composing a picture on-screen for your audience. Wear clothing and colors that work for you—that fit and are not distracting—and avoid too much white, which can cause on-screen glare. No tight patterns: pinstriped, checkered, or plaid.[4]

As is also crucial for in-person public speaking, do not put your notes in a ring-binder and flip the pages for all to see or hear. The resulting effect is unprofessional if not quite junior-level. Use a teleprompter or digital on-screen notes, and practice. As you do, keep making eye contact directly with the camera as much as possible.

Be Watchful, Perhaps Wary in Making Arrangements

As you begin to negotiate giving an online speech (as any speech), pay attention to the tone and spirit of your host and the preliminary contacts you make, especially if you sense the occasion will be quite interactive with the host and the audience.

If you detect any salient "vibes" that are troubling or quite negative, if you feel the situation could be very uncomfortable, awkward, even hostile, stop and think about it. If you don't feel comfortable with the host, the setting, or the tone of the occasion, and if you are not obligated to speak, perhaps you should back off and opt out as gracefully as you can, as soon as you can. Look for a better opportunity, or at least a better time to address the group, after you have more experience handling such a forum.

Not Your "Friend"

On the other hand, even if the host and the immediate audience are friendly, remember that an online appearance in itself "is not your friend." Mistakes can come back to haunt you, big time. For example, one major league baseball executive made careless, disparaging remarks about his team, and individual players—as if he were in an internal board meeting—while talking online to a rather small, public audience in the local community. The comments went viral! He got fired!!

Be positive, honest, thoughtful, and careful. Don't overreact to unnerving developments, and use good judgment in what you say. This is hard work, but you can get used to it, and reap many benefits for your work team and for yourself if you are careful and professional in the way you manage such opportunities.

In later chapters we'll get into further thoughts about issues and opportunities related to virtual public speaking, by way of in-depth interviews with two seasoned veterans about their experiences online.

CHAPTER 4

On Getting Invited to Speak

How do you get invited to speak at a worthy public forum—online or in-person—where you especially want to make an appearance? How can you be sure that agreeing to speak is a good investment of your time and resources?

Some invitations may come your way by happenstance. Sometimes you may feel obligated to accept. Yet your plans for public outreach should have more backbone than that. How can you open up opportunities to speak where it's advantageous for you and your organization as well as your listeners?

Strategic Plan for Public Speeches

Ideally, you or your communications, public relations, or marketing staff—or a trusted speech pro—should develop a long-term strategic plan for your public speaking. Without professional support you still can make good things happen yourself, but it takes a studied approach.

As a corporate speech coordinator often working with several executives in the same enterprise, this author framed the challenge to be "getting the right person to speak to the right group about the right subject at the right time in the right way with the right results." This actually summarizes the ideal mission of executive public speaking.

Your plan should spell out in writing, at least briefly, the strategic purpose of your public speaking, your goals, salient themes and messages, and at least a couple of measurable objectives—including key points of feedback—for each speech you give (we'll look at details about feedback in a later chapter).

Your plan should identify audiences and forums with a significant reputation in the community, their key contact personnel (typically, a program or event chair), good timing for an appearance, and major themes you could develop. Even though you need to be open to changes—such a plan is always a work in progress—all this calls for a disciplined approach.

Line up background information about such points as customer needs in the area, your enterprise's reputation in the community, problems and emerging issues, new business opportunities, changes in local management and operations, opportunities for favorable media coverage, and salient points for supporting the objectives and operations of your local team.

You need not put all of this into a long-term plan, of course. A few quick notes should suffice. It's the depth of thought that counts.

Clients have found it useful to see the plan as a one-page grid with appropriate columns, item abbreviations, and key dates (see Appendix 1 for an example). Once this is established, it's easy to share a copy with others, especially members of your marketing and public relations teams. Your associates would appreciate this.

Because you have many responsibilities and demands on your time, you may decide to speak monthly, bi-monthly, perhaps at least once a quarter. Typically, speaking fewer than five or six times a year isn't enough of a plan to deliver significant, tangible results over the long term.

One client, a regional bank CEO, preferred having a six-month scenario with speech dates once a month, adjusted and updated regularly. Another client wanted to speak only once a quarter. Yet the most ambitious chairman and CEO—the most successful in terms of overall career accomplishments, including serving on a variety of major boards at the national level—wanted to be out speaking to public audiences three times a month! And he did so with assuredness, poise, and great results.

Further Details for Speech Planning

For you, giving a public speech usually once a month may work well. The plan in Appendix 1 worked well for a midsize regional company wanting to speak to community service clubs and a couple of key business organizations. The results were measured by audience feedback, with metrics gathered by this author from follow-up with program chairs, as well as by media coverage if any, by comments this author gathered from attendees, and by observations by the local management team—especially about leads for new business. In this case, the CEO was outstanding as a speaker well-suited to the community audiences we targeted.

Yet for many top executives, this advisor has found that speaking only six-to-eight times a year is quite workable. Generally, this is sufficient to establish visibility, continuity, improvement in one's speaking skills, and a reputation as an effective public speaker. This also sets up enough of a record to secure opportunities at forums that have especially high standards.

Worthy Audiences?

For identifying groups worth speaking to, a good place to start if possible is with your management teams at the local level. They'll likely know, or can easily find out, which forums in their community have a good reputation and desirable membership, and would be worth addressing. Explain to your team that key factors to consider are business opportunities, diversity, inclusiveness, equity, responding to pressing needs, and fostering mutual interests in community development.

An approach that worked well for this author when dealing with remote communities was to get in touch also with the local city economic development office, or the head of a regional economic development council, to ask for help in identifying good speech forums, and whom to contact. Although such officials might be reluctant to give referrals, most gave good recommendations and, with further discussion, a useful perspective on current issues, the local economy, and new business opportunities.

Be aware that private, non-government economic development associations in small communities can be quite protective of their turf, and may not be too interested in helping an intermediary from out of town figure out local economic opportunities.

Media Coverage

An important factor to pay close attention to is patterns of media reporting about local business-speech events. There may be regular coverage at major forums, yet media contact is something to consider stimulating through a professional public relations, media relations approach. If you have a PR pro on staff, or as an ongoing advisor, take advantage of this.

Beginning to Listen First

When talking with leaders of public forums, a crucial step can be to identify names of recent speakers they've hosted so you could contact at least a couple of them to get their insights and suggestions for how to relate to that particular audience.

It also makes sense to find out who else is speaking in the general time frame you are considering, or at least who might be on the schedule before—and after—the date to which you would commit.

Check with your local team members or reliable local contacts to make sure all the planning fits together and makes sense before seeking and accepting an invitation.

In later chapters, we'll go into more depth about further ways to "listen first" before you develop your remarks.

A Quick Overview in Advance

In working with corporate CEOs and not-for-profit presidents or executive directors, this author has found that a crucial step is to give them a brief summary in writing for each recommended speech event—a brief memo. Ideally, this identifies the opportunity, why it is worthy, what the event or program chair expects, the general interests of the audience, opportunities for customer and media contact (and key investors also, if this applies), local team contacts to be made for additional background information, perhaps some key ideas, and suggested due dates for a draft of the script and for a rehearsal.

Even if you're preparing your own remarks, develop a summary like this for yourself in writing. Such a memo can be a sturdy launching pad and control factor for developing the speech, keeping it on target, and following up later.

Worth It?

Obviously, all this takes a lot of work. Also consider this:

If you don't believe it's worth taking the time to craft your message carefully and rehearse enough for a particular group, don't seek an invitation from them in the first place. If one comes your way and there isn't sufficient time to prepare, decline. Only accept invitations that you find to be worthwhile and if you have time to do the work adequately.

If you're not sure whether to accept an unsolicited speech invitation, review these points:

- Does it fit your strategic plan for public speeches?
- Is it a good opportunity to win friends, bring in new business, get publicity, overcome divisiveness, and enhance the reputation of your organization?

- Another crucial point is, will it help the members of your audience? By the way, if you don't see the location as a priority, and know you really can't do something meaningful, stay away. Otherwise the consequences could be trouble.

If the opportunity looks good, accept the invitation thankfully and prepare to do your best!

If you have a staff professional who can assist you with evaluating opportunities, developing overall speech strategies and tactics, and preparing at least a draft for you to work with, take advantage of this. If not, consider turning to an outside professional so you and your team can better invest your time in the day-to-day work you all depend on.

All This Seem Too "Corporate?"

If all this sounds too "big corporate," please consider that this author developed such speech plans for small-business clients in a proprietary "CEO Speakers Bureau." They included the owner of a business equipment leasing company, a branding and design professional, a business-efficiency management consultant, an executive coach, a marketing and branding professional, and the head of a forestry association. They wanted to connect with community audiences including service clubs, local Chambers of Commerce, and industry or professional forums. These clients found the visibility and in-person contacts through public speaking helped their business be successful.

In following the customized plan laid out for each Speakers Bureau client, they:

- Liked the discipline of speaking once a month,
- Appreciated a progression from small to larger audiences,
- Learned to present themselves more and more effectively as professionals dedicated to taking care of customers and serving the community, and
- Valued the connections and new relationships they established.

CHAPTER 5

Structure You Can Rely On

From the point of view of a seasoned counselor for a variety of top executives, it's apparent that the prime ingredient of effective leadership public speaking—for almost any talk—is careful use of structure—for in-person as well as virtual, online public speaking. Good structure is the key to being organized, fluent, interesting, even compelling. Let's explore some key points about this.

Ideal Script Format and Timing

In envisioning a well-structured script, for most occasions the following specification usually works best. Also indicated are the time increments which are ideal for many if not most speech occasions. Keep a copy of this for reference later.

Introduction	1 minute
Theme or "Thesis"	1 sentence
A. First Major Point	4–5 minutes
B. Second Major Point	4–5 minutes
C. Third Major Point	4–5 minutes
Summary—restate theme	1–2 sentences
Conclusion—call to action	1–2 minutes

In building on this foundation, for most in-person speeches the optimum goal typically is 17–18 minutes of speaking, 20 minutes maximum. This works especially well for a breakfast or lunch speech, and for many special-occasion speeches.

For a dinner in-person event, however, a total of 24–25 minutes—somewhat longer—has proved to be better, allowing for more examples, perhaps more humor or an additional personal story or two with a light touch and a more relaxed delivery.

Surprisingly, a longer time slot, such as a conference speech, typically scheduled for 50 minutes, requires only 35–37 minutes of actual speaking time. This allows for schedule delays and housekeeping announcements, introductions, and time for questions. In this author's experience, a conference speech seldom needs to be a full 50 minutes of material, unless a longer transcript is needed for business accreditation reasons.

If the event chair explicitly asks for 50 minutes—or if professional training credit rules strictly require 50 minutes of material—the requirement easily could be filled with examples, a case history or two, or additional personal observations supporting what you already are saying about your topic. (Also, it's always good to have extra material handy just in case you need to extend or restructure your remarks at the last minute.)

Such Structure Can Scale

Each of the three major points in the basic structure of your speech could have a similar three-fold substructure—three key elements supporting the major point. The "rule of three" in this case is not absolute, of course, but it does scale up and down nicely, opening up an approach that has an underlying natural appeal.

As an experiment, for a conference speech on in-store (grocery store) retail banking, this author once set up a perfectly symmetrical structured speech applying our format literally to see if such a touch would be noticed. In addition to the introduction, theme, and three main points, each of the three main points had three sub-points, all timed to be roughly equivalent in length.

When the speaker, not quite aware of the precision of the structure, returned from the conference, he was quite happy with how well the speech was received, saying he got several compliments, including how especially "logical" the speech was.

In general, a careful use of structure—although it doesn't have to be quite so evenly balanced, of course—is well worth your while.

Extemporaneous Remarks

If you are asked to extemporize at the last minute and "just say a few words," the structure of three main points still is a reliable way to go—just make sure the main points are relatively brief. State your theme and then take a couple of minutes to identify and support each of those three main points. That's a safe road to take. Typically, you'll be glad you did, and so will your audience.

Developing the Content

For building upon a well-structured foundation for your speech, the following chapters will explore how to develop your main points with insight, creativity, and effectiveness.

CHAPTER 6

Launch Your Creativity with Good Research

Once you agree to give a speech, and have an initial speech structure in mind, wouldn't it make sense for your next step to be to start drafting what to say as soon as you can?

No! Wrong. To begin working on your speech, the next thing to do should be to go back to researching the forum and the audience you are invited to address, so you can be responsive and successful. If you have a trusted public-speech adviser to do this preliminary work for you, take advantage of the opportunity. Otherwise, go ahead yourself.

Review the Situation

Consider the situation your potential audience is in. This need not be a technical analysis, but there are at least two levels to look into.

First, whether it's an address to a major civic group, a service club, or a professional or industry conference, make sure to check some basics about the forum itself. Talk further with the person who officially invited you, typically the program or event chair, and make sure you cover key points. Should the speech event be in-person only, or online, streamed for viewing at the listeners' convenience? Any particular requirements or restrictions (for example, no videos)?

Try to find out why were you invited at this particular time—why your topic is of special interest for the date you are invited. Is your speech part of a series with an overall theme? Is it related to a speech by someone else? In any case, be sure to ask who will have spoken to the group in immediately preceding months, and who's coming up after you.

You might ask how the organization is doing in general. Is it growing, changing, looking to achieve certain objectives? Is it trying to attract particular types of new members? Does the group leadership have an overall vision or theme for the current year that you should be aware of?

Also find out if there will be any additional program elements on the day of your speech—such as a holiday celebration, an awards ceremony, or one or more special guests for the day.

Check whether there may be internal or external news coverage (such as a newsletter, news releases for the media, recorded interviews related to the speech). Ask if the forum publishes material online, and whether they would like support materials (a photo, a bio, a quick summary of your remarks).

You also should ask if there are any expectations or caveats about the use of digital slides or video. Does the group prefer a speech with either no visuals or just a few—instead of an overall slide presentation? (Typically, presenting an outright "slide show" is not a good idea—too impersonal; we'll deal with this in more detail in a later chapter.) For visuals, what are the technical requirements? Does the organization intend to put your speech online?

Ask Particulars About Your Audience

Next, consider the personal situation of audience members. You may want to look into where they live, age and education levels, values and lifestyles, job levels, career situation (professional, median wage, retired), politics or topics of local community interest. You might wonder about their recreational, entertainment, and travel interests.

Further, are the members involved in any particular group projects at this time? Are they dealing with any major civic fundraisers or community goodwill activities? Above all, do they tend to ask the speaker a lot of questions? What kind of questions?

For a professional forum, a unique priority is to ask whether members of the audience need to earn accreditation points required by their professional organization, and if so whether a particular number of actual speaking minutes (including Q&A time) is required. Would special documentation (a topic outline, a certificate of attendance) from you be needed so your listeners could get credit?

In your preparation, it could be a good idea for you to actually attend one of the forum's sessions in advance of yours (or ask a member of your team to do so), and scout the situation. Watch how the introducer and the audience tend to relate to the guest speaker.

For an in-person forum, check how to use the lectern and mic, the shape of the room, the acoustics, possible distractions, and whether the overall atmosphere tends to be formal or very informal.

Transitional Stages

Not apparent but what could be significant is whether there are key transitions that the group overall, or at least several members, might be going through.

There could be a change of officers, or a membership or fundraising drive underway. Perhaps a change of venue is coming up. Maybe the group is looking forward to a seasonal break. Perhaps the group is on its way to achieving formal goals for growth. Or maybe they are ready to switch to or from an online meeting format.

Transitions of a different kind can include proven indicators of unique interests and information needs among members of any community group.[1] It could help you to know how many individuals will be in your audience:

- Occasional visitors or guests at the session you'll address.
- New members settling into the organization for the long term.
- Longtime members, perhaps thought-leaders who cherish the unique values and traditions of the organization, and who may have heard other speakers like you over the years. They may be more inclined to ask questions.
- Individuals looking to leave the organization and move on to another group soon, perhaps because of a job change or a change of residence.

Overall, you don't have to investigate so many factors, of course, but it pays to think ahead to some extent, and not just go on first impressions, with very little forethought about what might be happening with the audience.

As the cofounder and charter president of a traditional service club in the burgeoning Information Technology heart of Seattle, this author's job at the outset included inviting and introducing a wide array of guest speakers. It was apparent that few guest speakers "on the circuit" gave much forethought to such situational particulars. The speakers' talks too often seemed to be more about them and their pre-prepared message than about connecting with their listeners.

CHAPTER 7

Their Thoughts
and Your Thoughts

To go further into making your public speaking more effective, how can you focus on exactly how your audience may be thinking about your topic, or at least what their initial impressions may be?

Conversations

In addition to connecting with a program or event chair, try to talk briefly with two or three other representatives of the audience, such as committee members or past officers. Ask the event chair for their contact names and phone numbers. Typically, the organization's event or program chair will gladly help you identify good prospects to interview—if you just ask.

A useful approach in such conversations is, "If we could just sit down and talk about this [your topic], what might interest you, what might you be looking for, and what questions might come to mind?" If you have assistance available, you could ask a duly skilled associate or a speech professional to do this work on your behalf.

In general, this speechwriter has found that audience chairpersons, program committee members, officers or event coordinators are flattered to be asked to help the speaker, and are glad to do so, especially if they're contacted well in advance. Such contacts are welcomed because you are helping these officers be more successful themselves by ensuring that the guest speakers they bring in will be on-target, relevant, and interesting.

Your inquiries in advance may bring up topics to avoid as well as topics to cover. In such conversations you also may be reminded of good examples, even be reminded of a humorous story that could work. Most likely you'll be able to identify significant problems, interests, and emotions—and sometimes issues you would never expect.

By the way, what exactly is an "issue"? Usually this pertains to an information gap or mismatch that entails controversy. It may take some time to identify all sides of an issue you may want to or need to deal with, to get to what the missing elements may be, and to decide what exactly you could say that's helpful while avoiding undue controversy. (We'll deal further with gap analysis in a later chapter.)

Do the Homework

Your research may discover that someone else has addressed your topic already, or find that another speaker, perhaps with conflicting views, is invited to speak to the group for a program coming up soon. It's good to be aware of this so you can adapt, deal sufficiently with key counterarguments, and avoid being upstaged later.

Sometimes the individuals you talk with in advance may not be familiar with your topic at all, or—just the opposite—they may bring up difficult, perhaps technical questions that could be embarrassing or off-putting. They may be more informed than you assume.

Or if an interviewee does not have much to say, you could ask to be referred to someone in the group who is likely to ask questions, perhaps a chronic inquisitor you might as well find out about in advance. You don't want to get blindsided during your speech, or during Q&A at the end of your speech.

This author has been warned at least once or twice in the past about someone in an audience who likes to ask too many questions or dominate the Q&A period. If you're worried about how to deal with this, ask the program or event chair how other speakers have handled such matters. You might want to ask the emcee to help cut off a sharply pointed question or an attention-grabbing audience member by stepping in to suggest that the individual talk with the speaker after the event concludes.

As you gain experience doing such quick, initial interviews, you'll be more able to deal readily with ups and downs and special opportunities. If your timing is good, and if you are inquisitive and friendly rather than argumentative, your contacts will appreciate the conversation.

On a different level, perhaps the group is looking for a new cause to support in the community, and that's why you were invited. Or maybe there's a program that's important to them that you already support, and hearing you mention this they would be more interested in paying close attention to your speech in other respects as well.

Sometimes you may find you'll have to deal with audience members who really are "trouble"—who insist on seeing things their way, and will try to dominate any discussion. It's best to identify these challenges in advance and prepare for them, rather than get blindsided during your speech, or during the Q&A period.

A program chair once mentioned in advance that a regular attendee tends to ask challenging questions that annoy everyone. The chair noted where this person tends to sit. We practiced how to handle this with a short answer and an offer to discuss the topic at a later time.

Inappropriate?

Would such preliminary inquiries by you or a member of your team be unusual, "odd," or inappropriate? The person you are asking may be a bit surprised, even taken aback by your questions at first. It does take caution, a little humility, and some persistence to pull all this off smoothly.

Yet if you do all this in a spirit of co-questioning (more on this in the next chapter), this author's experience is that such contacts turn out very well, and are mutually appreciated.

The key ingredient in all of this is that if your advance contacts see that you are trying to do an especially good job, not just deliver a canned speech, they will appreciate your extra effort, and will want to support you in any way they reasonably can.

If you have a speechwriter helping you prepare, preliminary contacts by an experienced professional still can go very well. (This author has done this successfully many times for clients.) All the person needs to do is to explain that he or she is doing some research to help the speaker prepare. There's no need to discuss who's writing what. Individuals on the other side of the conversation likely don't care if you keep the focus on them.

Today's media-savvy public audiences generally are more well-informed than you might expect, and some may have deep preconceptions. Few will be sitting there with a "blank slate" on almost any business topic—whether it's your industry in general, wages and benefits, perceptions of climate change, the economy, equity, your organization's ideals and ethics, concerns about taxes, experience with your organization's products or services, your reputation as an employer, or any other business issue in your industry or in the community.

Be Responsive and Lead On

Remember that most audiences are kind—and they want you to succeed at least so they will feel good about the time they invest in listening to you speak!

If in your research you find that there's a concern or issue that is particularly timely or pressing, be sure to address it early in your speech—perhaps right after you get started, after the opening. Deal with it so you and your listeners can then go forward with you and focus on elements of your speech that strategically are more important for you to cover.

Pooling Their Thoughts: An Example

If you find in advance that your audience is especially talkative or knowledgeable about your topic, when you speak you might ask them to pool their thoughts and talk about that in a quick breakout session and report back to the whole audience!

One branding and design client, by then a well-seasoned public speaker after talking to a series of more and more challenging audiences, was invited to talk to a group of top marketing professionals about his firm's work on creating annual reports. To challenge the group and deal with preconceptions, he decided to break the audience into small groups early in his talk.

He gave each group five minutes to discuss the main message suggested by a collection of annual report covers the speaker's firm had created. Each group reviewed a different cover, and picked a representative to report on their ideas. People conversed, shared their thoughts, and reported back.

Usually each small group got the cover's message that the speaker's firm had intended, yet some reported useful thoughts even more interesting—in a good way—than what the designer expected.

In completing his talk, the speaker laced the groups' ideas together adroitly, skillfully using the audience's creativity to support his messages, and then added some unique perspectives of his own. Everyone learned something new. It all was refreshing, and effective. The group loved it, and it was another win for a favorite client.

Questions at the End

It's crucial to leave enough time at the end of your speech for audience response in a question-and-answer period—for your own sake as well as theirs. This takes discipline. Too many—if not most—business speakers talk too long and cut off priceless engagement time at the end.

In reaching out to community audiences, it's so important to "listen" as well as to respond. Everyone can learn from Q&A, including you if you are open-minded.

If you don't have all the answers at the moment, you can get back to people by making feedback sheets available at the end, so that respondents can write out their questions and comments for you to reply to later. Such an approach can enable you to follow up—and could lead to mutually desirable business connections.

Timely Considerations

Seasonal factors may pertain—holidays, the end or start of the forum's fiscal year, group or club elections, recognition of new officers. On the day of your talk you may find there are special guests or public figures attending, a brief memorial for a member who passed away, showcased entertainment by a student group, concern about a setback for the group, and attention to industry or political news or events that relate to your talk. You might encounter lingering feelings about a recent speaker, perhaps someone who made jaded comments that clash with your very topic. Finally, there may be heated politics or infighting going on among members of the group that might affect you, your topic, and your approach. Check it out as best you can in advance.

CHAPTER 8

Secret Sauce:
Questioning Tactics

Consider a new approach to preparing and presenting speech material that's a bit deeper and can work especially well: tactics for co-questioning. This is a matter of creative thinking on your part as well as probing more sharply how people tend to think about your topic. With this, let's also reflect a bit on how you can use co-questioning to add unique flavor and zest to your speeches.

Like any special sauce, this may take a little patience at this point to unlock and appreciate the secret.

Real-Life Example

The following is an example, edited somewhat, of a co-questioning dialogue taken from one of this author's past "CEO Speech Doctor" emails to clients and colleagues. The point here is to pick up some of the actual remarks in the featured interview. With this in mind, we'll then get into how to apply underlying, science-based concepts that are the foundation of such an approach.

Welcome to Speech Doctor

In framing an upcoming speech, some of your key building blocks can be the interests, problems, and issues members of the audience bring with them as they listen to your speech. Seldom do you have a blank slate to write on. So how do you know what will be in the room—the information needs of your audience? Check it all out beforehand, at least to a reasonable extent, using what we're calling the "Co-Questioning" model.

How to Co-Question

In working on two related speeches for a telecommunications client in the past couple of months, actually several weeks in advance, I've learned some points that I'd like to pass along to you. In this case I was only handling "placements"—getting the client invited to speak, and setting up some basic logistics.

The client intended to develop his remarks himself, which was to be about the future of the telecommunications industry. I endeavored to provide plenty of lead time for this speaker. We had collaborated on a similar speech previously, so it seemed the upcoming speeches could be mostly a matter of updating old material. Not so.

Findings for the First Speech

I contacted the program chair for the first group to see if I could ask some background questions. I was wondering about what the audience members may have on their mind, questions they might ask during a Q&A session at the end of the speech. I also asked if there were a couple of additional audience representatives I could talk with about the upcoming speech.

His response: "I'll have to think about polling some of the members about the talk. We have never done this, but it's a great idea.... Thank you for your thoughtfulness about this." (I appreciated his enthusiasm.)

He suggested I contact a previous member of the forum's program committee. This one said, "The audience is broad, lots of business and non-profit leaders amongst many sectors. I'd suggest staying high level.... This would be as opposed to going deep or technical on any one topic."

As I continued the conversation via email with that person, in the back of my mind I was wondering what patterns of inquiry (co-questioning) might come up. The speech topic was a general overview of the speaker's industry. It seemed this could spark the listeners' curiosity in many ways.

I did not intend to go into the many thought patterns that could be pertinent, but it helped to have more particulars in mind than just blind curiosity. As a professional I believed I should have more on the ball than just relying on intuition.

This person's next response was: "I always go back to, 'What's in it for me and why should I care?' As an attendee, I'd like to know how all of this innovation will improve my quality of life in the coming year, what are the new or ongoing privacy concerns, and what we as consumers can look forward to in the future."

What struck me was the comment about privacy, something the general public, especially businesses and professionals, was getting more and more concerned about. Also apparent was a call for imagining—at least foreseeing, if not predicting—some things that could evolve in the industry's future.

Findings for the Second Speech

The client's second speech was to be a conference keynote on innovation, focusing on how the speaker's industry relates to advances in small manufacturing operations. The request was for the speaker to address how his company's technology could help foster innovation in manufacturing, and to discuss management strategies for helping any company be more innovative.

In speaking to the chair for this event, I found he wanted to meet with the speaker in-person to talk about all this. A generous offer, not too common, which in this case could help the speaker tie into topics other speakers would cover at this event. They eventually did confer, at least briefly.

As for my part during that initial interview, I realized there also could be some interest in the speaker's company as an investment, and for particulars about the company's financial performance. So, I pointed this out to my client, and he agreed to prepare for this.

Does Co-Questioning Help?

I've found that this "co-questioning" approach—identifying and blending the audience's interests and thoughts with your own as a speaker—adds value to a speech all around. Thoughtful, professional contacts in advance by a speaker or speechwriter, instead of just "winging it," can make all the difference in crafting a successful speech.

Co-Questioning as a Concept

To anchor all this on a deeper level, consider the "behavioral molecule" developed by communications scientist R.F. Carter.[1] Wanting to better understand communication as units of behavior, he turned to the image of a behavioral molecule, and envisioned the molecule as having three parts: "Questioning" (in the sense of broad inquiry), "Defining" (as in selecting a course of action, or shifting gears), and then "Moving" (taking action).[2] Carter's breakthrough work[3] inspired this researcher-author to focus on the behavior of questioning[4] to examine how readers and audiences resolve their information needs (my original, primary motive for pursuing advanced studies in communication theory). The overall structure of the molecule is summarized below:

"Behavioral Molecule": Questioning + Defining + Moving

Thus, for anyone preparing a speech, as we've alluded to already, the place to start is questioning—to be understood here in a broad sense of inquiry. This can help us think through what we might cover in a speech and how to do so, particularly if we can get down to useful details.

Building on a tradition of classic co-orientation communication research,[5] let's therefore take a closer look at co-questioning ways and means as the road to getting a firmer grip on how we can lock in with listeners to communicate effectively. Consider all this as a mutual endeavor to identify specifics about what the audience may be thinking already, build on those specific elements, and coalesce them with the unique insights you have to offer.

A "Questions" Speech

A somewhat rough-hewn, quick example of all of this is a talk this author gave in person to a small service club about speechwriting. They were wondering what it's like to be a speechwriter, and invited me to speak. With an easel pad, marker pens, and plenty of painter's (non-marking) tape handy nearby, my opening thanked them for their interest in speechwriting, and asked them what questions they might have in mind.

They quickly got into it, and raised a variety of pointed questions, which yours truly wrote out and posted on the wall of the meeting room.

The next step was to thank them, turn and look through the questions for a moment, and reorganize the sheets of paper according to three main topics, and then give a speech addressing the questions in that order. This was easy for me because of a depth of experience, and none of the questions were particularly surprising.

The speech was responsive to their interests, engaging, and we all got a kick out of it! At the end of my 20 minutes, in asking if there were any more questions, it turned out everyone seemed to be satisfied. They apparently liked the speech, even were enthusiastic. But no one came up afterwards to say they really wanted to be a speechwriter!

The point is that applying a spirit of co-inquiry, co-questioning, by doing audience research in advance and being open to listen and learn from the audience before you speak can (1) energize your remarks, (2) help you truly engage with your listeners, and (3) engender a worthwhile outcome for everyone involved.

Remember that the group already has asked you to speak. It's okay to ask at least a couple of them—at least your host or the program chair—to think through the topic with you in advance. They may not be used to it, but invariably your questions will lead to fruitful conversations. Above all, such preparation can put you on track to an especially good outcome.

Thought Patterns as "Questioning Tactics'"

This co-questioning approach can take us to considering several specific ways of questioning, "Questioning Tactics,"[6] that you could select as main or supporting points of your speech. These tactics originally included Trial-and-Error, Searching, Following, Screening, Pointed Questioning, Judging, Seeking, Problem Solving, Checking, Hypothesizing, Discussing, Debating, and Decision-Making. We'll take a closer look at these and more on the next few pages.

Many such patterns could apply (the possibilities are unlimited), but some are quite predictable. One tactic frequently dealt with in public speaking is "Problem Solving." Many a speech deals with a problem, noting key aspects of the problem, what led to the problem, and thinking through perhaps jointly with the audience how one or more new solutions makes sense. Another typical pattern is "Following," as in following key trends in an industry, or in the economy in general.

One more tactic is "Seeing Opportunity," identifying a positive condition or development in what looks like a negative picture to begin with. You'll find several more Questioning Tactics listed below and specified in detail in Appendix 2.

It's important to note that these tactics can be mixed and matched in a variety of patterns. For example, drawing from the list in the appendix, "Seeing Opportunity" could include a series of Searching, Imagining, Discussing, Experimenting, and Judging. "Remembering" could include Pointed Questioning, Screening, Reflecting and Discussing. "Imagining" could include Remembering, Checking, Seeking, and Decision Making. Problem Solving could include several tactics in more than one sequence. Finally, in a particular instance it could be crucial to note the similarity and differences between Imagining and Hypothesizing.

On Getting to "Co-"

As you begin to consider such thought patterns, let's be clear and restate what should be going on. Your intentions are key. Your challenge is to explore how to connect with the audience in terms of their way of thinking, and then bring them along with you into your speech material so they can relate to what you present, and more easily reach the conclusion(s) you intend or propose.

Interests, Concerns: The Audience's Point of View

So let's spell out some initial patterns of thought that may characterize your audience:

- Are there any specific, pointed questions the audience may ask?
- Would the audience be searching for factual information related to your subject?
- Do they tend to follow key sources of information—including particular thought-leaders—about your industry or at least your general field of business?
- What issues or controversial elements might they ask you about?
- What choices or decisions might your audience need to make about your topic in the near future?

Identifying such ways of thinking may be essential to connecting with the audience and reaching a mutually satisfying conclusion about the topic you're addressing.

Intuitive, Inviting, Collaborative

At this point you may agree that the phrase co-questioning has an intuitive ring to it, a sense of good intentions, a feeling of invitation, a note of humility, and an openness that makes your speech be an occasion for you to put things out on the table for everyone to see what makes sense. As one advisor put it, "Approach public speaking as the sharing of ideas as well as a business."[7] The resulting co-inquiry can be creative, powerful, and convincing.

Questioning Tactics: Tools for Developing Your Speech

The following, therefore, are some patterns of thought you could look for, and perhaps choose to develop in your speech. For *definitions*, see *Appendix 1*.

- Checking
- Clarifying
- Confirming
- Debating
- Decision-Making (choosing)
- Depicting
- Discussing
- Envisioning
- Experimenting
- Following
- Forecasting
- Hypothesizing
- Imagining
- Inspiring
- Judging
- Pointed Questioning
- Praying
- Problem Solving
- Probing
- Reflecting
- Remembering
- Screening
- Searching
- Seeing Opportunity
- Seeking
- Testing
- Thanking
- Trial and Error
- Visualizing
- Waiting

Options at Your Command

Think about these patterns of inquiry as options in your playbook for developing your speech. You could take one of the above thought patterns to use as your strategic, overriding approach for the speech, and then choose other items from the above as tactics for developing your thoughts with three major points. In other words, depending on your topic, you could choose any one of the items on the list above as the basis of your "strategy," and develop and support it with a mix of tactics, perhaps three as the basis of your three major points.

This is a unique capability that can sharpen your thoughts. Be creative—and keep the spirit of "co" in all this, reflecting on audience interests, perhaps challenging preconceived notions, and introducing new, creative, dynamic ideas.

Examples

In a speech about how to deal with the local economy, you might base your outlook on (1) "remembering" overall economic patterns over the last decade as well as seasonal differences you've seen lately, then (2) identifying reliable sources you are "following" today and why, and finally (3) "judging" or weighing alternatives you anticipate, and then selecting one of them.

In another case, as you think about what to say, you may sense that your audience would enjoy "imagining" a new approach with you. Perhaps they'd be interested in talking in small groups ("discussing") for a few minutes to compare notes, as in the annual reports example in the previous chapter. Then you could get into "testing"—how the group could test out, at least in an informal experiment, what you have in mind.

Being Informative

You may notice that the thought patterns considered above suggest not only being inquisitive but also being informative. This is particularly useful when your message is stoked with a sincere interest in the audience, when you're trying to foster a positive outlook, and when you have new insights, perhaps "big ideas" to deliver.

CHAPTER 9

Spice in the Sauce:
Empathetic Outreach

Some time ago, during advance speech research for a new client scheduled to give a university commencement address, a colleague of his mentioned to me how the speaker had great "emotional intelligence." This is a term originated by science journalist Goleman[1] and that has evolved into a popular mix of concepts, procedures,[2] and advisory services today.[3]

The client was a company-division president who was asked to speak at the university's winter-quarter graduation ceremony. He was a past graduate, and a faithful and supportive alum. Given the situation it was clear that emotion as well as ideas could play a huge part not only for the speaker but also for his audience of students, parents, relatives, friends, faculty, and staff.

This was at a time when the outlook for jobs and the economy in general was not too encouraging. So delivering a positive and realistic message would be a challenge. It helped that he also was a parent of teenagers, at least somewhat familiar with rock music and youth culture in general.

We succeeded in developing a worthy speech, but it was not easy. The rest of the story is spelled out in a future chapter.

Was this occasion truly unusual? Don't most executive speech events deal with facts and evidence much more than emotion? On the contrary.

During years of corporate and independent speech work. This author has seen or worked with executives speaking in a variety of highly-charged emotional situations, including:

- A newly-arrived chairman and CEO, with 20 years of CEO experience at a larger bank, taking over a failing regional bank being saved by the FDIC. His debut included addressing the bank's management team about prospects for the bank's recovery and for keeping their jobs—in the context of major reorganization and upcoming layoffs. Fear hung heavy in the air, and the tension and anxiety in the room were palpable.

45

- A statewide division vice president of a major telecommunications firm addressing a memorial service for employees and contractors killed in a landslide while working on buried cable along a steep ridge overlooking Interstate 5, in a severe mid-winter rainstorm. Shock, grief, suspicion, sorrow, and sadness hung heavy in the air.
- A regional bank chairman speaking to a family-oriented community audience about life lessons she learned from her grandfather.
- A marketing senior vice president speaking at a holiday event to his division employees after an especially successful year.
- Annual meetings dealing with a wide variety of emotions, some pleasant and some very unpleasant.

You probably can recall emotion-laden speeches you've experienced as a member of an audience if not as a speaker. How can an executive speaker like you best deal with all this?

Emotion in a Speech vs. a Presentation

The opportunity if not the need for dealing with emotions is a key difference between an informational "presentation" and the leadership public speech. Typically, in speaking to a community audience you're not just delivering information, you're also expressing—in positive or unintended negative ways—your care about your listeners, your personal interest in the community, and your organization's dedication to positive linkage with the community. It's business—and it is personal.

If you are interested in achieving a good effect on your audience regarding such points, consider an age-old principle from the Greek philosopher Aristotle, the "Father of Rhetoric," who suggests that positive effects "may come through the hearers when the speech stirs their emotions."[4] (We'll see more about Aristotle and the wisdom of ancients in a future chapter.)

Typically, speeches you'll give about your industry, company policies, and the community are largely informational. Yet you want and need to inspire trust and workable conditions if not also public support for your businesses and your industry in general. You may have to deal with the ups and downs of divisive politics, hostile listeners (see a future chapter about dealing with the unfriendly, perhaps hostile audience), and instilling enthusiasm for your business and business-related community events.

Emotions if not evident as you prepare a speech may be waiting in the wings to stride if not rush onto the scene as you begin to speak.

So how do you prepare to deal with emotions in a public speech?

Respect

First, let's raise a couple of preliminary, pointed questions. Overall, while you hope for respect from the audience, yet is respect for them a top concern for you?

What is respect anyway—a thought or an emotion? The literature is rife with definitions, distinctions, quotable quotes, specifications, research, essays, and advice. Clearly the need for mutual respect is essential today given the dysfunction that runs rampant in our society—racism, sexism, generational biases, status aloofness, arrogance, divisiveness.

In a public speech forum, the dynamics of respect start with the speaker. Make respect your top priority. Keep respect for your audience top of mind.

Empathetic Outreach

In considering emotions, the early notion of emotional intelligence has led to a plethora of biomedical and social science research on empathy, or "the ability to share in and understand others' experiences vicariously."[5] A framer of that definition more recently noted that the term, empathy, has become "multidimensional, interpersonal, and modulated by context"; and that medical neuroimaging has identified "neurocognitive mechanisms" that underlie different aspects of empathy; and that "cultivating empathic concern" at least in medicine is especially important.[6] "It's a fact that some people are better 'hardwired' for empathy than others."

Empathic concern is highly valued in management circles. For example, for college and university presidents, empathy is seen as "an intangible trait that separates and defines the leadership of the best presidents."[7]

In speech preparation even though we may not be able to examine audience emotions in detail—we're not talking about gearing up for therapy here—it should readily be apparent that it's wise to get some sense of the emotional situation of your listeners before you speak to them.

Given this, to accompany our behavioral molecule for co-questioning, let's consider another new behavioral molecule, Empathetic Outreach, with three parts: Discerning, Focusing, Relating. we'll refer to this new behavior molecule repeatedly,

----

Empathetic-Outreach Molecule: Discerning + Focusing + Relating

----

In this context, "discerning" audience emotions can include asking the program chair, event chair, conference chair or forum leadership in advance about the emotional climate of the group, about any particular feelings, perhaps regarding seasonal changes, special events, major challenges the group may be dealing with, and especially in regard to your organization and your role in it. Discretion in inquiring about this is essential, of course, but it can be done.

As you go forward in developing your speech, "focusing" on particular sentiments directly may be appropriate. At least you should be aware of the potential for stirring up problematic emotions. It can be especially beneficial to tune into good feelings.

In "relating," you may want to acknowledge problematic conditions perhaps by telling a story that addresses the feelings of the audience—for example, dispelling animosity or encouraging positive resolution.

As carefully-designed research has shown, expressing empathy "particularly with strangers" can require hard work.[8] Yet, again, we're recommending making at least a reasonable effort to be sensitive and responsive.

The Range of Emotions

In trying to discern emotions, what could you be watching for? In his classic work on rhetoric, Aristotle envisioned dealing with such emotions as calmness (as the opposite of anger), friendship and enmity (hostility), confidence, shame and shamelessness, kindness and unkindness, pity, and indignation.[9]

One resource in social science literature about emotions is Plutchik's classic list of eight primary emotions: joy versus sadness; anger versus fear; trust versus disgust; and surprise versus anticipation.[10] A more thorough list was identified in a recent behavioral study by Cowen and Keltner[11] that examined self-reports of emotions experienced by subjects viewing a number of short video clips—which were intended to depict thirty-five emotions. Their list included the following items:

- admiration
- adoration
- aesthetic
- appreciation
- amusement
- anger
- anxiety
- awe

- awkwardness
- boredom
- calmness
- confusion
- contempt
- craving
- disappointment
- disgust

- empathic pain
- entrancement
- envy
- excitement
- fear
- guilt
- horror
- interest
- joy
- nostalgia

- pride
- relief
- romance
- sadness
- satisfaction
- sexual desire
- surprise
- sympathy
- triumph

This list is a bit daunting, but the point is that there could be a lot of emotions stirring "out there" as you speak.

Pay attention in advance to emotions that seem to be especially pertinent to feelings about you and your organization, your topic, and thoughtful inquiry that may come up. In considering the tides of emotion today, it's especially important today to be careful about comments regarding religious, ethnic, gender, and individual differences that drive emotional response.

Misinformation, Racism, Sexism, Hostility

Today, given the divisiveness stemming from a global pandemic, racist turmoil, human-rights issues, and mass shootings, along with warfare in eastern Europe and major geopolitical tensions, most of us are aware of the tides of emotion that can engulf our communities. For public speaking, consideration of emotions can be crucial in whether you (1) try to get invited to speak, (2) decide to accept an invitation, (3) attempt to identify audience assumptions about who you are and what you believe, (4) assess their dispositions, and (5) prepare sufficiently to deal with troubling if not hostile remarks by audience members, at least during a Q&A period.

In thinking about how to speak about emotions, consider (1) developing tactics to maintain, intensify or reduce an emotional response, (2) managing your own emotions, (3) paying attention to the emotional reactions of your audience as you speak, and (4) engaging with audience emotions in ways that are natural for your listeners and can readily support what you are trying to communicate.

Communicating Emotion: What to Do and Not to Do

One helpful perspective on all of this comes from a seasoned coordinator for TED Talks, who advised:

Craft your talk with the language that your audience speaks. For example, if you're speaking on a panel, you can speak more intimately to the audience. If you're at an event that's more high energy, your language can reflect that—you can entertain the audience a bit more. If you're at a conference that's for professionals, you can speak in more technical terms. Speaking the same language as the audience increases the odds that they will hear you, understand you, and be inspired by you. You're more likely to connect with them emotionally.[12]

Be cautious, however, about using current "in" words and popular expressions, because missing a detail or using an expression that's off-target or out of date could be disastrous.

If your audience and the occasion is at least somewhat oriented to entertainment, or is generation specific, even a few quick references to relevant artists, songs, concerts, or movies—familiar arteries of emotion—could add a unique depth of emotional communication. Intuitively recognizing that music is a primary language of emotion, the commencement speaker noted above effectively made reference to a rock band (Death Cab for Cutie) the students knew well, to good effect.

It also may be useful to consider shareable memories of names, places, and events your audience could appreciate. You could mention your personal roots, if any, in the particular community where you are speaking, or your own experiences with the type of work or organization you are addressing.

The main point is that such efforts to tune into the experiences and emotions of your audience will win you feelings of kinship, confidence, and support.

Careful Yet Caring

At the same time, be careful not to be boastful, or express annoyance, disapproval or undue anger, especially about anyone in your audience, even though such feelings may be quite tempting. Your audience likely will pick up on and remember negative, angry, racist, sexist, or other put-down comments much more readily than any rational argumentation you present. Your negativity could be all that they'll take away from your speech.

On the other hand, it makes sense in a business speech to a public audience to show authentic passion for taking care of customers, for delivering your best in products and services, and that you feel strongly about doing what is "right." Your audience will pick up on your sincerity, appreciate your dedication, and likely will be all the more receptive to the rest of your remarks.

Many if not most organizational audiences you address aspire to published values that are heartfelt, attract new members, motivate group activities, and are heralded in the group's achievements. Ask around. Look for such documentation either on the group's website or in published material. This applies to service clubs, industry associations, chambers of commerce, professional associations, educational programs and institutions.

With a little research you can identify heartfelt values, and then acknowledge those values and traits at least briefly in your remarks. Appreciating such values and briefly thanking your audience for their work in supporting such ideals can lead to recognition and appreciation for any similar activity by your own organization.

For business speeches one public relations manager always fostered a dedication to "taking care of customers." Her sincerity about this was inspiring, memorable, and effective.

In commencement addresses speakers typically mention the values and traditions of that academic institution. Service clubs have key slogans, stated values, and traditions that, when recognized and endorsed by a speaker, promote a strong, positive response and appreciation by the audience. People like it when a speaker supports what's dear to their hearts. A little of this goes a long way, yet with sincerity this is sure to elicit a positive response.

Emotions and Q&A

Discerning audience emotions can be essential as you handle a Question-&-Answer session following your speech. If a strong emotion is evident as someone raises a question, perhaps indicating animosity toward you, your company, or your industry, acknowledge the emotion carefully to show you "hear" this. Avoid any expression that could be taken by the questioner or the audience as disrespectful, unduly argumentative, or arrogant on your part. Do mention relevant evidence of what your organization is doing to correct a problem. At least acknowledge an intention to look into it—if you're sincere about that.

It may be wise to ask the questioner if the two of you could communicate further about this after your speech. Be careful not to over-commit and then walk away. That could come back to haunt you.

A useful tactic in general to deal with questions is to make copies of a one-page informational handout—including your contact information—readily available, perhaps online, or in-person near the exits, so anyone could leave you a question or comment along with their contact information, or at least be able to contact you later, after the speech. You might want to mention the handout at the outset of your Q&A session, particularly if you realize there isn't much time left for questions.

A "Combination Reaction"

Referring back to our physical science analogies about behavioral molecules, consider what can happen in combining the molecules of co-questioning and empathetic outreach. The result can be like a chemical "compound reaction." In chemistry, depending on the molecules being combined, the reaction can result in the release of energy as heat, or absorption of energy as cooling. For a speech the point here is that combining thoughts with appropriate emotions can make a big difference. Show them you care!

When the "emotionally intelligent" client combined a focus on co-questioning with his skills in relating to audience emotions, the result was evident. His combined use of questioning tactics and empathetic outreach resulted in a heightened level of energy and response that was effective, convincing, and memorable.

CHAPTER 10

Put It All Together: A New, Dynamic Model for Executive Public Speaking

Before we go on to particulars about how to develop and deliver an executive speech, let's step back and envision the major steps recommended for producing a speech that meets your needs, the needs and interests of your audience, and the leadership expectations of your organization's team. The rest of this book will drill down on how to research, write, internalize, rehearse, deliver, and evaluate a speech online or in-person.

Consider the diagram below showing the recommended seven-steps approach for developing a public speech. So far, we've examined steps 1 and 2, which takes us to researching your audience, as explained in the next chapter. Thereafter we'll examine the remaining steps and consider further guidance.

Seven Steps Up to Public Speaking Success

7. Evaluate via Feedback

6. Deliver

5. Rehearse

4. Write, Develop Visuals If Any, Refine

3. Audience Research

2. Structure Main Ideas

1. Seek/Accept Invitation

Interview to Gather Particulars

Given the above considerations about questioning tactics and emotions, the next step is to begin to develop perspectives on thoughts and emotions by actually interviewing the program or event chair, or a similar audience representative. Your objective should be to learn what you can about the situation you'll be in, what may be going on with the audience you'll be facing, their interests and concerns, how people might react, and aspects of your topic that may be particularly relevant or sensitive—so that you can prepare your remarks accordingly.

Then, as you wrap up that interview, try to get contact information for at least two more representatives of the audience whom you could interview in order to get some diversity of opinions. These others could be members of a program committee if there is one, or for a conference, members of the conference planning committee. Ask the program or event chair for suggestions for whom to interview.

The Guided Interview

To optimize those opportunities, prepare an "Interview Guide" with questions you can ask for fine-tuning what you should cover or stay away from in the speech. Keep your list of questions brief. In the calls you make, probe for good answers. You want to learn enough to be so responsive that your speech can become "a shared vehicle for communication."[1]

If you see that particular emotions are a key factor, you may want to interview at least a couple more individuals representing the group to hear more. Ask questions discreetly, and make a point to listen carefully to what comes up. Listening (and taking notes) is the hard part. Don't take your listening skills for granted—listening is hard work.

The following is a sample interview guide for making such a call yourself about a speech you'll give.

Introduction:

Hello, this is _____ of _____. I'm calling about my upcoming speech at (name of the forum) on (date). Thank you again for inviting me to speak, I'm very much looking forward to being there with you....

May I ask you a few questions about the speech? This may take a few minutes, perhaps fifteen minutes or so. Is this an OK time for this? (If not, reschedule.)

- Before we get started, do *you* have any questions you want to ask me at this point? (Pause.)
- Thank you.

Key Questions to Ask:

1. So my intention is to address _____ (topic or title of the speech). Do you have any particular thoughts at this point about this topic and what it might include, or at least what I should touch on?

2. Have you had *other speakers* address this topic, or are there any *other* speakers you've scheduled to talk about this topic in the near future?

3. Are you aware of any particular *interests* or *questions* you might suggest I cover?

- If so, *what might be of particular interest* to the audience?

4. *Anything else* you might suggest I deal with?

5. How do you think your group will *respond* to a speech on this topic—any particular reactions, comments, or points of interest?

- Anything more?

6. Is your group dealing with any particular *issues or concerns* related to this topic at this time?

- (If appropriate:) Can you tell me more?
- How do people in your group tend to feel about these things?
- (If needed:) Can you tell me more?

7. In a Question-and-Answer session at the end of the speech—I hope we'll have time for this—are there *any particular questions* that might come up?

- Anything else?

8. Is there *someone else* in your group you could suggest I talk to regarding all this—maybe someone you think has a particular point of view?
9. *Anything else* come to mind?
10. That's all at this point.

Conclusion: <u>Thank you</u> for your time and your thoughts!

Note 1: As you go along in such an interview, be sure to probe if appropriate for further responses, asking "Anything more?" or "How do you yourself feel about this?" (This pronoun grammar is intentional—in market research it helps draw out useful responses in phone interviews.)

Note 2: After you've completed two or three such interviews, you should have enough material to go on to write a speech that is personal, responsive, and can benefit everyone involved.

Note 3: See Appendix 3 for a simulated example of a conversation using a simple interview guide with an executive director of a major, international conference. This is meant to give you a further sense of how responses in such a conversation could be helpful for fine-tuning a script and accompanying visuals.

CHAPTER 12

Write Inside Out

For actually writing your speech, let's review some "inside" considerations, and then reflect on getting it "out" on paper. This is an approach that works for me and many others, and it may help you as well. The first step is to structure the progression of your main ideas, the core of your speech, in your mind, or even better, write them down. Then reflect not only on your overall theme and major points, but also on the flow and the feel of your material.

Develop Major Points

As the speechwriter for one particular CEO, this author prepared many speeches by using the following sequence of questioning tactics. Such an approach often may work for you:

- Remembering: recalling familiar, in-person features of retail delivery systems used widely in the speaker's industry.
- Screening: referring briefly to delivery systems used by competitors.
- Problem-solving: typically, this can be broken out into a number of steps. (More recently, communication scientist H.S. Kim identified key steps for community problem solving.[1]) In the speech, the CEO abridged the process and quickly got to the solution the company came up with.

For problem-solving in a different speech, a CEO explained how the company went back to customers, listened more carefully to their service frustrations and needs, and then pulled together new technology and new incentives for improving those customer services.

For your speech, with your major points in mind, develop an outline. In one complete sentence summarize your overall theme, the main thought of your talk. Follow that with one key sentence for each of your major points (ideally, three, or four at most), and then a one-sentence summary restating the theme, and finally a one-sentence conclusion.

Reflect on what you have. Does this outline say what you want? Do your major points invite the listener to stay tuned? Are they clear? Does your speech overall hang together and amount to something new, interesting, and memorable?

Go Beyond Bullet Points

A seasoned public relations manager once said, "I've often wondered why CEOs or upper-level executives will spend hours working on a sales pitch and presentation, but write a bunch of bullet points on a dog-eared piece of paper and then go out and try to speak effectively to a large number of people. They wouldn't be giving the speech to begin with if they didn't think the audience was important."[2]

From a business point of view, the notion that "all I need is a few bullet points" truly does not make sense. Too often the result is a somewhat awkward, halting, off-the-mark speech that disappoints everyone involved, wasting everyone's time and a valuable opportunity.

What's Wrong with Bullet Points?

What can go wrong?

First, you may say something "off the cuff" that you'll regret later. We've all seen top leaders go wrong with a careless remark that did the speaker and the company no good. If there are reporters, investors, and customers in the audience, wrong words can get you in trouble. Anyone with a smartphone could make a video of your talk that could go viral, at least record what you are saying.

For yourself, if you later believe you are misquoted, without a script you will have no record of what you actually said, or at least meant to say. On sensitive matters, as an executive, it's always best to know clearly what you intend to say.

Second, your speech may fail the basics of well-balanced structure and thoughtful co-communicating—carefully relating to the ideas, interests, and emotions including concerns of the audience in a fitting sequence.

Third, if you only have bullet points, you may forget details that add life, spark, and quick understanding about what you are trying to say. You may be reminded about and mention unnecessary matters and lose the emphasis you want. You'll likely take too long, cutting off Q&A time. It's always best to leave some time for interacting with the audience so you can respond to them—and so you can learn something from them!

Fourth, if you actually have a script, you could hand off copies to media representatives covering your speech to help them report about your speech, to help make sure the coverage is accurate.

Writing is difficult. Not everyone thinks and creates the same way. For some of us, if not most, a systematic approach on paper can make a positive difference. Do your best.

Get Writing: A Head Start

By the way, if you find yourself intending to write your speech tomorrow for an upcoming deadline, take a moment today to start today, before you quit for the day. Jot down some key words for the introduction, the theme, the summary, and your conclusion. It's all right if your notes are quite sketchy. Even a few quick notes today can work wonders.

The next morning you'll find those notes will put you miles ahead for a full go at completing the writing. This is much better than having to start a new day cold, facing a blank page, struggling to get your creative engines going. At least such a head start works well for some of us.

Write Start to Finish?

On the contrary, some writers do best if they start from scratch and write their whole speech from beginning to end, scripting away. This is a rare talent. Certainly, few if any of us are as quick and definitive in writing as an Alexander Hamilton, who reportedly[3] was accustomed to starting cold and scribing perfect text page after page, and could write volumes this way. Most of us likely are better off starting with a sketch on paper and then working to flesh out our text, and touch it up to make it better.

Rules for Conversational Speechwriting

Keep in mind the following guidelines, along with clear awareness that you are writing for the ear, if you want to achieve an effective, conversational style:

- Stick with simple sentences, and keep them short—but not all the time; variety can be good.

- Use familiar terms, but also ramp up your imagination and challenge the audience's usual thinking.
- Go for lively verbs in the active, not passive, voice.
- Use colorful examples, avoid boring clichés.
- Overall, your speechwriting should be more about the audience than about you.
- Use informal yet executive-level language; no off-color expletives, no insider "company" jargon, no acronyms unless it's material familiar to everyone in the room.
- A tone of humble self-confidence usually is best. Arrogance will come back to haunt you later.

True Test

Smart, lively script-touches can make a speech work and sound better. But better in terms of what? First of all, the executive speech doesn't need to be a matter of polished words and oratorical excellence—which could be distracting if not dysfunctional anyway.

You may notice that in this book we're not focusing much on classic figures of speech, eloquence, or formal oratory, although there is nothing wrong in any of that if it fits you and the situation.

The door to useful figures of speech is always open. Classic Greek rhetorician Aristotle suggested the use of similes, metaphors, homonyms (similar-sounding words), apothegms (concise sayings), and proverbs. Another he suggested is antithesis, introducing two opposites together for contrasting effect, such as John F. Kennedy's—as drafted by speechwriter Ted Sorensen—"Ask not what your country can do for you, ask what you can do for your country." That wording is classic.

The true test of a well-scripted executive speech, in my view, is whether in delivery the speaker's remarks are consistent in style and tone with the way the person comes across afterwards in answering questions. "One speaker, one voice" is the goal: being consistent is the key rather than a mishmash of style and techniques.

Be yourself. That's what got you invited to start with. That's what has taken you to the executive level. So be authentic.

Pretest

The best pretest to assure a good outcome for a speech is to read it aloud to yourself at least once, then again to a willing listener, and make any needed changes as you go. Rehearse at least one more time with the same person or, even better, a different, perhaps more critical listener.

Edit carefully. When in doubt, simpler phrases and shorter wording usually are best. Keep it conversational, especially for an online speech.

There are singular benefits from rehearsing in front of someone, especially practicing making at least some eye contact as you go. The reality of this helps you fine-tune the pace, the timing, engagement, and the "feel" of your remarks.

Too Time-Consuming?

Does all of this take too much time? It is work. Yet with practice you'll pick up personal shortcuts along the way. You'll become more and more efficient.

Rehearse during the fringes of the day rather than during appointment or work-session sweet-spots on your calendar. You're likely to get more rehearsing done this way, and your speech preparation will feel less burdensome.

Consider this: If at first you realize that you can't take the time to prepare for a speech well enough, decline the invitation, or at least postpone the commitment. A public speech makes a lasting impression, so give yourself a break if necessary. Otherwise, brace yourself and do the work. Once you commit, give it your best effort, be your own best friend for the long term, do the best you can.

Long-Term Payoff

A favorite CEO client gave an average of three public speeches a month, including practices, with ease. He followed the aforementioned rules (well, he did have a dedicated speechwriter). Nonetheless, he reviewed prepared remarks in advance, usually making only a few changes, and practiced on his own.

Most especially, in delivery he learned from experience how to "read" a script with lively dynamics—just as a seasoned actor with little preparation can deliver a well-written script smoothly, with good eye contact, and with a lively spirit of engagement. I'm convinced that almost anyone—that you—can learn to do this.

This particular executive was a favorite client because he always was dedicated to excellence, and enthusiastic about helping others by offering useful ideas. He was widely sought after to be on corporate boards at the regional and national levels, and peer executives in other industries admired and respected him and his work. Sometimes one would wonder how he could do it all. He was one of the most accomplished executives this author has ever known.

The point for you is that, as with other performance skills, the more you work at public speaking, carefully following tried-and-true procedures, the more you'll feel confident and be sure of yourself. And the process will become easier and much quicker. Your speeches will be more and more satisfying for you and for everyone involved, especially for your audiences and for the team you represent.

CHAPTER 13

Put a Face on It, Tell a Story

As a new CEO observed, getting people in the community to care about one's industry and business is a challenge. This executive's concern was that most businesses need the support of the community not only for sales, attracting new team members, and keeping employee families healthy, but also to provide sturdy infrastructure, safety, and keep taxes at a reasonable level.

When speaking to community audiences the key is to put a face on your industry and your company, and personalize your remarks to make them "real."

A Story

One way to do so is to tell a story when pertinent, and to work it enough to make it interesting. Include some color, imagination, and even some fun. Doing so works better than just presenting impersonal facts and figures, charts and graphs, analyst reviews, and testimonials. Give examples from your personal experience, from real-life situations.

Why?

Giving your listeners a slice of life is personal, believable, and convincing. This, by the way, is another key way a good "speech" is different from an informational "presentation" designed for training, for a staff conference, or for the board room. To build a relationship with a public audience, tie your remarks into the everyday, down-home experiences your audience cares about. Good stories can get the job done.

"Giving your listeners a slice of life is personal, believable, and convincing."

You may be familiar with Abraham Lincoln's Gettysburg Address. So brief. So powerful. So perfect. Yet anyone who looks more deeply into President Lincoln's usual style of public speaking will see how frequently he used stories—a lot of them—to make a point. A voracious reader as a youth, he also was an incessant storyteller: "Almost from the beginning his classmates admired his ability to tell stories.... In their eyes he was clearly exceptional, and he carried away from his brief schooling the self-confidence of a man who has never met his intellectual equal."[1]

In his early campaigning days, when politicians would give drawn-out, entertaining stump speeches for as long as two hours at a time, Lincoln made generous use of his story-telling repertoire, piecing together from his early days as a frontier rail-splitter, a river-boatman, and a circuit-traveling attorney working with clients from all walks of life. In campaigning for president, he combined "his remarkable gifts as story-teller, and teacher ... with a lucid, relentless, yet always accessible logic.... Lincoln used irony and humor, laced with workaday, homespun images to build an eloquent tower of logic."[2]

Even though President Lincoln in informal conversation sometimes took too long with friends—he was a rambling storyteller with guests at the White House[3]—in speeches he usually drove home his views efficiently with stories that slipped into listeners' imagination, understanding, and memory.

Even today, there is something quite engaging about a somewhat "storytelling" style of speaking, especially at a dinner or festive event when there's more time available. For such situations, the use of down-home anecdotes—if you keep them brief—is highly recommended. Audiences like to share in the color, the feelings, and the wisdom that stories can impart.

"Audiences like to share in the color, the feelings,
and the wisdom that stories can impart."

A Close Relative's Advice

A story about learning from a parent or a respected elder almost always gets attention. Consider this story, about taking a broader perspective, from a widely respected client who represented a major nonprofit in her in-person speech at a university commencement:

If you told me my most important mentor would be my grandfather, I would not have believed you.... He was quiet, usually reserved. He didn't say much. One day as a teenager I was surprised to read an interview of him. He told a story about a flute player. The man practiced his flute every day, but his playing did not improve. So, he sought my grandfather's advice. Grandfather told him to stop playing the flute for a while, and, instead, go out and find ways to help his friends and neighbors. Many weeks later, the man called my grandfather to thank him for the advice. The musician said his playing was, indeed, much improved. At first, I thought the story did not make sense. But the more I thought about it, the story became a metaphor for me. I am task oriented, and tend sometimes to lose the forest for the trees. But when I can step outside of myself, like in the story, I am able to grasp "the big picture."

Learning from a Parent

Another kind of story that almost always gets attention is giving an example of especially insightful instruction from a parent. It's sometimes surprising how well we learned about life from them in many ways—too often despite ourselves. One major executive related what he had learned about sales and customer service working as a youth in his golf-pro father's shop. As the story went, a customer wanted to buy a particular set of golf clubs. The budding young salesman, however, tried to explain why the newest technology would be better for the customer, how it would be a much better choice.

Seeing that the customer was getting uncomfortable with the conversation, the father interceded, and quickly closed the sale on what the customer wanted, wishing the buyer all the best. After the door closed, the father explained that the customer had his own reasons for buying. While it was not bad to point out the latest developments, the pro said, the son needed to focus on the customer's wishes.

That story about a lesson in the back corner of a golf shop was a new way for an audience to appreciate at least one reason why the speaker was able to lead his business team to success. The story helped make it evident that the speaker and his retail team emphasized putting the customer first—convincingly. And from the point of view of a customer, this author could tell they were good at this.

Being a Parent

The following comments remind us that sometimes business and family responsibilities go hand in hand—particularly for a family-held business. The speaker was the chair of a forest products corporation (the remarks are edited somewhat for anonymity). For a moment he spoke as a father, and the audience appreciated every word:

> I represent the fifth generation of the family, and all the family expectations that go with that. So good stewardship of forests for the future of our company and for the future of the region is something I bear in mind every day. I think about this as I pry the sixth generation of "shareholders" out of bed in the morning, or engage in an impromptu "shareholders meeting" over a holiday dinner.

A Touch of Humor

Especially effective can be a relevant story that's truly funny. If you are not a gifted comedian—few are, and many a joke backfires—a safe and effective way to proceed is to tell a brief story where the joke is on you. Consider this tongue-in-cheek example from a speech given by a financial services chairman and CEO speaking to a major service club during an economic recession:

> After the financial services bubble burst ... the banking industry had been mostly on the defensive, dealing with a lot of problems. As you know, a lot of negatives, a lot of criticism, a lot of public discontent. And I know that many people still question the integrity of our industry. In fact, things got so bad that one day, during the heart of the darkness, I even called my mother and apologized for growing up to become the president of a bank. She really helped me put things in perspective when she explained that it was okay because, quite frankly, she never expected much of me anyway!

Self-deprecating humor is a safe bet. A little humility goes a long way. This particular touch of humor gives us a clue as to why this CEO and his conservative team had sailed through a banking crisis relatively unscathed.

The All-Out Humorous Story

It takes nerve to tell a story that entails some acting-out with a colorful touch of personality, but it can work. With some encouragement, a newly promoted president gave storytelling a try after some prompting and with a little coaching. A top executive in a major Midwest city had asked the speaker—at the time a Northwest official in national account sales—to come and see him about a business matter. So, as the story unfolds, the speaker flew in and took a cab to the prospect's downtown skyscraper headquarters. As the self-assured salesman began to get out of the cab, however, he scraped one of his shoes on the curb, totally knocking off the shoe's heel!

At that point, he said as he related the story, he could just see himself hobbling into the customer's office, feeling and looking foolish. Usually especially well-dressed, he was distraught, figuring this customer call would be quite embarrassing, to say the least. Yet he paused, and reminded himself that the sales call was not about him, but about the customer—a customer with a need that apparently only this Pacific Northwesterner could fill.

So, in concluding the story, he said he braced himself, forgot about his problem, and focused on taking care of the customer. Successfully.

This all came about because when this speaker was promoted to president, he was given speechwriting support and speech training to go with it. During one training session, with an additional trainer/coach that this author recommended be included (for an outsider's perspective), the new president happened to mention the "shoe" incident. We encouraged him to act out the story in his next speech, and with a little coaxing he agreed to give it a try. He told the story, was pleased how well it worked out, and told it again on several more occasions.

Telling such a story not only helped him be more comfortable in speaking, but also made his speeches entertaining, endearing, authentic, and memorable. Usually unflappable anyway, and quite outgoing, his portrayal of the incident proved to be hilarious. His audiences loved the story.

This client went on to become a speaker in high demand, able to engage with his audiences with great confidence—he even looked forward to giving a wider variety of speeches. His creative, imaginative business practices (for example, initiating a successful "5 minutes or $5" cash payment policy for anyone having to wait too long in the bank's service line) and his spirited talks led to many worthwhile speaking invitations that came his way. Along with this, he revitalized a company that needed a positive and energetic outlook, engaging vision, and confident leadership.

Give Situational Examples

Another CEO client occasionally was asked to speak about the state of Washington's economy. He was especially knowledgeable, and not only knew the numbers but also spent a lot of time meeting with and listening to customers in a variety of industries.

For a major speech our plan was for him to tell a brief story—as a situational example—about each of a few major sectors of the region's economy. This writer's job was twofold. The first was to prepare economic overview material by checking with this writer's network of economists up and down the West Coast (the job also involved tracking key issues, the economy included). The second, and more interesting effort meant contacting the company's relationship officers to identify an appropriate customer in each of a few industries we selected. The bank's regional teams got permission directly from these customers to interview them so that the speaker could quote what they had to say about their industry, albeit anonymously.

In speaking about the agricultural sector of the state's economy, for example, the CEO talked about consensus forecasts, and then zeroed in on the true-life challenges the head of a family farm faced, as well as opportunities they saw for their business. Such a reality check delivered insights about a segment of the economy not well understood by a "big city" audience.

Later the state's official economist contacted the CEO, and ended up talking with this speechwriter. He had heard about the CEO's speech and the situational examples. He wanted a copy of that speech for his own reference, as well as copies of any similar speech material we might generate in coming months. He explained that he got all the usual reports, records, and forecasts from economic analysts, and studied all the numbers, but he rarely got to hear "the inside story" on what's happening, as covered in this CEO's speech.

For executive public speeches, such research and storytelling can pay many dividends. The customers identified and interviewed for the economics speech appreciated the company's special interest in their business, their industry, and their way of life. Good customer relations! This was in line with the company's head of Public Affairs strategy to make "taking care of customers" a top priority, and energizing and supporting that priority day in and day out.

Predictable Success, a Sense of Community

Stories carefully chosen and well-crafted almost always work well for the speaker and the audience. Audiences like to share in the color, the feelings, and the wisdom that stories can impart. Above all, such personalized outreach pulls everyone into a closer sense of how much we all have in common, thoughts and feelings we share, how much we depend on one another, and how we can help one another as a community.

Fine Points

CHAPTER 14

Virtual Speaking to Major Community Audiences

For a candid view of what it's like for a top executive to speak to a virtual, online public audience, let's turn to a seasoned executive[1] who has served as the regional chairman of a nationwide bank, serves on a number of corporate and not-for-profit boards, and is a predominant, highly sought-after speaker at major public forums throughout the Pacific Northwest, and at business and industry events at the national level as well.

1. What do you see as the key differences between giving virtual, online speeches as compared with traditional in-person speaking to community audiences?

"All of my speeches today are online—on Zoom or Microsoft Teams, Zoom to Zoom, or Zoom to an in-person audience. Not one in-person speech, although this will change. The differences I see are technical, structural, and in terms of relationships.

"With every device you use, you have to pay a lot of attention to where the camera is, usually have to stand up. It's always important to work with the technical staff on where the lights are, my eyes, how my face looks, how I am presenting my material. It is really hard to work with no 'live' feedback from the audience.

"As far as structure, we have to do a lot more work getting in touch with the audience. Before, when we could see the audience, a speech could flow more congenially, with more natural interest. Today everything is so much more structured. We have to work hard to engage with the audience. I feel I spend a lot more time getting ready, structuring the content, varying the tone.

"In terms of relationships, before, especially in a panel discussion, we could call on one another, and get feedback; it was much more collegial. In talking to 150 people online, you don't feel the connections, you can't see how people are reacting. You don't really have relationships as before, speaking in-person. You feel very disconnected. You can't watch for signs of questions, read their body language, can't notice gestures, can't see their faces. There's no way to get to know people. Even for people you do know, you can't really see their reactions. That's really tough."

2. What's most difficult about giving a speech online?

"Occasionally I teach classes, for example on 'governance,' to an Executive MBA group. Used to do so in-person, but now it's by Zoom or Teams. It's just very different. Just talking is a whole different thing. You want to feel that people are listening and following. But you're not sure they get it. I'm not sure I'm as effective as I've been in the past [face-to-face].

"Looking ahead, there will be more in-person speaking as we get past the pandemic, but online speaking will be with us from now on."

3. Let's talk more about the technology. What are some key factors you have to deal with?

"Lighting. That's critical. You have to make sure the light is in front of you. Make sure it's the right light—ring lights, for example. In advance you have to make sure to pay attention to the background, that it's not too distracting. You have to make sure you're looking directly at the camera, so that it all comes together.

"Before beginning, you have to spend 5–10 minutes checking exactly how your voice sounds, what the overall effect of your appearance is, the net effect of what you are projecting."

4. What works to get the audience more involved, to keep their attention?

"You don't know what questions they might have. It would be good if you could ask questions, but almost everyone is on mute. So, it all tends to be less personal. I try to smile more, slow down a little more, to pause, to look like I'm trying to read the audience. It would help to see their eyes, their expressions—all that is a good thing."

5. What do you like to know about the audience in advance, if anything in particular?

"I do think that, for Rotary, for example, if you know some in the audience, it would be good in advance to field some of their questions. Usually you don't know if you would have access as you speak. As you speak everyone needs to be on mute.

"Could ask the host to do a little research for you."

6. What helps you feel like you are getting across to people on the other side of the camera, as far as their receptiveness or reactions?

"Again, it's very hard to look at a screen as you are talking, listening as you are talking. It's much easier if you are onstage and can also look at the [live] audience while you are on camera, to relate to people in the audience."

7. As you look back, what do you especially value about the whole experience as a speaker, what are some benefits about speaking online?

"It's a very efficient use of time, on schedule.

"The reason I continue is to get my messages out. I feel very strongly, and passionately, about a lot of things. The general topics that are close to my heart are community, diversity, and inclusion, good governance and leadership.

"I like to engage with audiences and get their feedback, especially if I feel passionate about the subject."

8. A "best" online speech?

"For me a 'best' speech is when I believe the topic is worthwhile, I get my message out, and get feedback. For example, when I talk about diversity and inclusion."

9. Summing up, what is the most important lesson you have learned about the difference between in-person and online public speaking?

"A speech before Zoom was about building a closeness, a capable sense of community. I enjoy that.

"It may be more difficult to relate online, it takes work, but we can be proactive, put challenges out there, challenge people to make a difference, and show that we're in it together.

"It's more important than ever to research your audience in advance. Including 'pre-fielding' questions in advance."

10. Anything else?

"My sense is that there will be a 50–50 split on online versus in-person public speaking.

"The worst speakers will be the ones that come across as knowing-it-all. It's hard to convey a bit of humility; however, we all should be working at it.

"The best speakers will make sure to find out why they were asked to speak, and what questions and [interests] will be especially important for the audience. Be proactive!"

CHAPTER 15

Virtual Speaking to Smaller, More Interactive Audiences

The following interview[1] features a longtime CEO of a major design firm who today mentors a wide variety of young creatives in marketing, design, and technology. He has a long track record of accomplished public speaking to in-person and online forums at the local, national, and international levels.

In addition to advising a wide variety of clients and coaching young professionals, he writes extensively on the challenges of doing business in this era of rapid changes in technology and major opportunities for product and service innovation.

The context here is the use of videoconferencing platforms to speak to public audiences large and small. This speaker often has addressed classroom-sized groups as well as much larger audiences.

1. What is the key difference today between giving an online speech versus traditional in-person speaking to audiences in the community?

"Online you're all in small, individual rectangular boxes, so you don't have the kind of experience as when the speaker is up front at a microphone and everyone else is seated together in the audience. The speaker's box is the same size as everyone else's. This elevates the audience to the same level as the speaker.

"Also, you have 'chat.' So, individuals can type in a question or a comment while you are speaking. This way you can invite members of the audience to contribute to the conversation. You can get their participation and attention that way.

"In a virtual situation you don't have the kind of separation that there is in-person. Everyone is on the same playing field. All in the same size, little boxes. It's a big difference!"

2. What's most difficult about this?

"When people in the audience turn away from their cameras or turn them off, it's very obvious they are not engaged. That's very hard on the speaker.

"Video software doesn't let you see all the little cues you can see when speaking to a live audience. The downside is that it is hard to read the audience. We are very attuned to a raised eyebrow, to facial gestures communicated by those tiny muscles of the face.

"The software of video does not communicate everything to the speaker. In video not everything is visible. Another disadvantage online for the speaker is the fatigue that comes from trying to read someone in the audience and the information just is not there. We have had the same problem when speaking live to an audience wearing masks.

"There's no difference between a meeting, giving a formal speech, or simply having a meeting. For the speaker it's all the same."

3. Let's talk more about the technology. What are some key factors you have to deal with?

"The technology always is changing. Sometimes things don't work. Everyone goes through this experience. Trying to figure out what's wrong is very frustrating. The speaker is nervous, and people get angry. It's difficult to get yourself back in your head.

"I've had the experience of getting my earbuds synched with my phone but not synched to the computer I'm using. Sometimes people are looking at multiple screens, and their headphones may be synched to a different computer.

"And there are so many systems that are different. Skype, Google, Zoom, Teams. People switch systems.

"What do you do? You try to be patient, to put it all together."

4. What works to get the audience more involved?

"One of the educators I work with requires that the class answer specific questions about my talk. She gives me their feedback. That's a great benefit because it helps me see what works. Two things: stories, a good story well told, especially any kind of story that ends in a failure, not success. And any kind of exercise that gets them to negotiate with one another. I use the 'chat rooms' feature for that."

5. What do you like to know about the audience in advance, if anything in particular?

"Why they are interested in the subject. I'd like to know if they could tell me about a situation that's related.

"I talk to a group of writers on collaborating, improving our writing. I know from experience that creatives can work together. I want to know their background, their experience, the settings they've been in, their personal interests. I like to know what they read, what they are inspired about."

6. What helps you feel like you are getting across to people on the other side of the camera, as far as their receptiveness or reactions?

"Nodding in agreement, signs of affirmation. If they are interested enough to ask questions so it all relates to them. Practical questions, not theoretical questions. Something where someone describes a situation and asks how they could have dealt with it differently, how to deal with particular situations."

7. As you look back on a particular virtual, online speech, what do you especially value about the whole experience as a speaker, particularly speaking as the CEO of your company?

"Being relevant to people. If what I have to offer is of benefit to them. Are they interested?"

8. Speaking as an advisor to business colleagues and young professionals, what do your virtual, online listeners really tend to like?

"The technology and COVID change things so much that references to the past can lose people. Yet what's been important for 350,000 [*sic*] years still applies. Our human behavior was shaped by experience, by a history of working together before the agricultural revolution. We're desperate to be 'in the group,' be appreciated, be relevant. All these fundamentals are just as true now as back then. We're not very well adapted to the kind of world we live in today. We've not had time to adjust."

9. In a "best" virtual, online speech, what went especially well?

"What I always remember is when people ask a lot of questions— you know that people are engaged."

10. So how could you take advantage of that in advance?

"By reading past reviews, what people wrote about what went well. That's how I especially learned the value of stories."

11. Summing up, what is the most important lesson you have learned about the difference between in-person and virtual, online public speaking, in terms of your being successful as the featured speaker?

"Know who you are talking to. Get information about them in advance. Develop stories that are on target. With a smaller group, have some kind of exercise people can do. If possible, break them into subgroups. If the audience is too big, ask for some volunteers and put them into a chat room to come back and report to everyone.

"To foster engagement, tell a problematic story, such as how to deal with a protest—a dramatic story."

12. Anything else?

"You have to watch and see if your audience is following you. If not, be ready to change what you're talking about. You need to have different takes on your subject matter. You've got to engage—such as with a story about when you just about failed and you pulled it out, and survived.

"The fundamentals of how you appeal to your listeners will never change, making connections will never change.

"Bring up questions. Asking is far more effective than telling."

Note: In retrospect, how is online speaking by a guest speaker, a business leader at a community forum, different from an online meeting with peers in offices or working-from-home? What's unique is the setting, the status of the speaker, and that the audience typically is a mixed group of people who are not used to working together. For such a situation—and the thesis of this book in general—it's possible to make connections as a guest speaker if you do the homework needed to tune into your audience's agendas, interests and concerns. Developing succinct examples and stories can be crucial.

CHAPTER 16

Create Smooth Transitions

Even if you think you only have time to write out a few elements of your speech—one would hope they're expanded with as much good text as you can muster—at least add transitional words and phrases to the beginning of each key point. This fosters smooth and clear delivery.

Let's assume you take the time to develop an overall script structure, writing out complete sentences at least for the opening, for the main theme, for three major points, subpoints as well, and for a summary and a conclusion—the structure recommended in Chapter 5. Maybe you intend just to speak from an outline. In any case, go back and be sure you include a transitional word or phrase where appropriate, at least at the beginning of each major point, to lead fluidly into what you want to say.

These major transitions can make all the difference in helping the audience keep in step with you. Otherwise, it will be apparent that you did not do your homework, and as one executive observed about his delivery, your speech will seem to be "too choppy."

Transitional Words

Need some examples of good transition material? The following are typical expressions you could use in a speech, especially as you make a transition from one major point to the next major point. (These terms are listed by topic in alphabetical order, for your convenience):

- Acknowledging: although, still, be that as it may, after all, even so, and yet, nonetheless.
- Addition: also, as well as, at the same time, besides, beyond that, furthermore, in addition to, likewise, on top of that.
- After: and so, as a result, as a consequence, consequently, later on, therefore.
- Before: first of all, before that, let me take you back (a favorite), looking back, could see that coming when, what led to that.

- Certainty: beyond doubt, clearly, evidently, for sure, indeed, to be sure, unquestionably.
- Comparison: instead of that, in the same way, on the contrary, on the other hand, likewise, more importantly, much the same, rather than, similarly, what's more.
- Conclusion: all things considered, it comes down to this, thus, since these things are so, in conclusion.
- Example: as a case in point, for example, for instance, in my experience, in particular, like, such as.
- Generalizing: as a rule, by and large, in general, more often than not, most of the time, ordinarily, overall, usually.
- Optimism: assuredly, encouragingly, looking on the bright side, I'm confident that, I'm encouraged that, I expect.
- Redirection: at the same time, besides, by the way, incidentally, not to mention, speaking of that, that reminds me.
- Sequence: after that, along with that, at this point, finally, first, next, to begin with, with that.
- Summarizing: all in all, all things considered, in a nutshell, in essence, in other words, in summary, it all adds up to, to sum up.
- *Note*: Avoid the tiresome phrase "the bottom line"—it is quite off-putting, especially for a community audience.

Visual Transitions

You also can add a personal, visual dimension to your transitions. For in-person speeches, if you are limited to having a lectern mic, you can use body motion and gestures to make transitions. For example, change your eye contact as you begin a new point—perhaps to look at a different part of the room for a few moments. If you have a stationary microphone, as you turn to one side or the other, move your head so you still speak "across" the mic instead of away from it. Turning away can reduce the volume, and you'll lose the audience.

Keep in mind this sharp, on-point advice: "If the audience is large enough and a microphone is required, make certain that you stay in front of it. Directional mics can be death for most non-professional speakers."[1]

If you are able to use a portable ("lavalier") microphone for an in-person speech, change your position from time to time, even walk to a different area on the stage if you can—particularly when you change from one major point to the next. Yet as noted previously, do not pace back and forth—a common fault. If you keep it up, the audience may start rooting silently for you to walk right out of the room!

For an online speech, making such visual transitions is more difficult. It may work to change your body position somewhat, but always keep good eye contact with the camera.

About Slides and Video

If you need to use slides, make sure the slides are for support only—not to deliver your speech for you—and make certain your transitions into and out of each slide are well-paced and smooth.

A key point in all this is commonly violated, especially by tech executives speaking to community audiences. A start-to-finish show of slides or video to a public audience is not a leadership speech. Such use of slides, virtually or in-person, by a top executive looks quite junior-level. People expect eye-to-eye insight from an industry leader. For a leading executive, the general public isn't looking for a teacher, they would like to know you, gauge your way of thinking, and hear directly what you have to say.

Slides may be appropriate for boardroom presentations, but even then the slides should be just for support—charts, illustrations, and data—not "be" one's talk. A great but sometimes intimidating executive this speechwriter worked with while he was a Chairman and CEO reportedly would kick a staff presenter out of a board meeting if that person "read" from slides instead of maintaining eye contact with the board members. He wanted every presenter to address the board directly as an authority on the matter at hand. He wanted his direct reports to know their material readily, to know what they were talking about!

Similarly, in a public speech to a community audience, for an online talk or in-person, using too many slides—and too long a video—can be quite off-putting, an obvious "crutch" detracting substantially from the personal impact of such a speech.

People want to know the story directly from you, not from canned material.

If you truly need to use slide data or images as part of a speech, make sure the graphics have a professional, consistent appearance (easy-to-read fonts, harmonious colors, simple design and layout, strong images). If you can't afford top-quality visuals, whether video or photos, don't bother.

Finally, if and when you do use visuals, be sure to prepare and practice using appropriate transitional words as you change images so the audience can understand what's happening, and can follow you easily.

Engagement as You Speak

One authoritarian CEO knew that he tended to look "owly" (his term), rather harsh, as he got deep into his subject matter. In informal conversation he usually was quite friendly, and engaging. Yet public speaking wasn't his greatest strength. Without being aware of it as he spoke, he could get quite intense, even look a bit threatening as he discussed complex ideas, was laying out the way he wanted things done, or was trying to lead the audience to new insights.

Realizing this, and wanting to truly engage with his audience, he occasionally would write in the margin of his notes to "smile," as a reminder to relax and ease up a bit, particularly at the beginning of each major point in his speech, to reconnect with the audience. He didn't always succeed in mellowing as much as he might have wanted, but he tempered his authoritarian tendencies, usually seemed outgoing enough, kept the attention of the audience, often was quite inspirational, and always was worth listening to.

As a side note, on the job his command presence was intentional, at least to some degree. One day he confided to me that he was careful to manage his "stature" this way because he thought it was best for his role, his team, and the company in general. This executive expected and got top performance from his direct reports, was held in high esteem throughout the company, and truly was a memorable—and gracious—client.

Adjust Your Tone of Voice

If you notice from feedback you get, or in reviewing a video of one or more of your online or in-person speeches, that you tend to drift into a boring monotone as you go along, work on it. Vary the pitch and speed of your voice. Variety of tone is good, and it's particularly useful as you make a major transition. Make a point to inject new energy into your comments when giving examples, and, for an in-person speech, in changing your position on stage.

In Summary

The whole point of using good transitions is to make things easier for the audience to follow you, and for you to change gears with renewed energy. If you put a little thought and extra effort into your transitions, your audiences will be glad you did, and they will be much more inclined to stay with you throughout your speech.

CHAPTER 17

Sharpen Your Writing

When it comes to sitting down and writing your speech, consider a few advanced scripting touches that can help your public speaking sound and work better.

Coherence

Overall, if your prepared remarks and the way you answer questions afterwards sound the same, your script fits you quite well. If not, the following structural and style touches can make a difference.

Your Language

First, remember you're writing your script material for the ear. What usually works best is using simple words, short sentences, and informal language. When it's essential for technical or legal reasons, however, to use terms unique to your work, do so sparingly.

In speaking about finance, science, engineering, health care, or information technology, for example, it's easy to lose your audience. Avoid insider jargon as much as possible unless you are sure everyone will understand it readily. Skip the acronyms, simplify your expressions, give down-to-earth examples.

Once again, consider the classic advice of Aristotle: "Style to be good must be clear.... Clearness is secured by using words that are current and ordinary ... disguise [your] art and give the impression of speaking naturally and not artificially."[1]

We'll hear more from Aristotle in a future chapter.

The "Power of Three"

A structural device that can work wonders for almost any speech is what some call "the power of three." Such structure can apply in matters large and small, including at the micro level, phrasing.

For threefold power in phrases, a classic example is "faith, hope, and charity." For broader thoughts, consider the word-pattern in Abraham Lincoln's address in 1863 on a battlefield near Gettysburg, Pennsylvania: "We cannot dedicate, we cannot consecrate, we cannot hallow," which as one commentator put it "had a solemnity worthy of the occasion."[2] Although his political campaign "stump" speeches sometimes were three-hour marathons, the 272-word "Gettysburg Address" consisted of three paragraphs!

As a side note about this, legend has it that Lincoln jotted down his remarks on the train to Gettysburg, or even that he composed it on the spot. Actually, he did the work in advance. As historian David Reynolds points out, several days before the train ride Lincoln showed the speech to a colleague who had been a member of his cabinet. Lincoln also told a journalist, Reynolds reports from a key source, that he had "written it over two or three times," and said he would "give it another lick before I am satisfied."[3]

He was preceded at the lectern that day by noted orator and former president of Harvard University, Edward Everett. After the event, Everett wrote to the president, "I should be glad if I could flatter myself that I came as near to the central idea of the occasion in two hours as you did in two minutes."[4]

Once again we see "the rule of three" can assist us greatly in preparing a speech:

- In developing a major point—introduce three key sub-elements, such as three key facts, or three quotes, or three examples.
- In a short story you tell—limit it to three quick elements to make it brief but substantial.
- If you name references to support your view, a quick-list of three can be convincing.

A Deeply Rooted Tradition

Perhaps in a high school history or Latin class you took note of Julius Caesar's "veni, vidi, vici" ("I came, I saw, I conquered"). Mathematicians foster the power of three in setting up proportions. Musicians young and old practice and feel the power of chord triads. Some scholars trace the Rule of Three to theology (the Trinity).

At some point you've likely heard of Winston Churchill's "blood, sweat, and tears" (his actual words were "blood, toil, tears, and sweat," but his admirers usually recall the pattern of three instead).

Order Counts

Not so evident at first is how to make a combination of three elements—large or small—especially powerful. In an editorial writing class years ago, a senior journalism professor and media veteran, John L. Hulteng,[5] recommended putting the strongest element last, the second strongest first, and the not-as-strong in the middle. In other words, "better, good, best." This is a powerful arrangement.

What's ideal, however, can vary by situation. For example, in the early afternoon it may be good to wake up a drowsy audience by making sure your major first point is your strongest and nails down everyone's attention.

More Combinations

For the speeches you develop, for your major points keep in mind such patterns as past, present, and future; the situation, the problem, and the solution; pros, cons, and recommendations; what works, what doesn't, what's ideal.

By the Numbers

There's also magic in how to set up a longer list of items you may want to mention. You may like "Top Ten Lists." Also, a list of "five" tends to work better than four or six. Another approach that generally works well is a list of seven. Consider the question raised by classic psychologist G.A. Miller:

> What about the magical number seven? What about the seven wonders of the world, the seven seas, the seven deadly sins, the seven daughters of Atlas in the Pleiades, the seven ages of man, the seven levels of hell, the seven primary colors, the seven notes of the musical scale, and the seven days of the week? Perhaps there is something deep and profound behind all these sevens, something just calling out for us to discover it.[6]

Restated as "Miller's Law," his findings along with related information-theory research suggest "the magical number seven, plus or minus two" can be useful guidance for us. In general, for our purposes, all this suggests a list in a speech might be best with five to seven, perhaps even 10 items. If you're tempted to go for more, don't do it!

Extra Effort Pays Off

In considering such fine touches, take note that making a good effort to use a few basic structural devices can make your speech more effective—and memorable.

CHAPTER 18

A "Show" Within a Show

In an in-person executive speech, it indeed can be good to use a few audio-visual elements to illustrate key points, but you should continue to be in charge, rather than just relying on your audio-visual elements to speak for you. Your challenge is to be the continuity yourself, and lead a positive "conversation" with the audience directly. A-V material should just be for illustration. How can you keep this in balance?

A Special Main Point

One way to deal with this information-and-relationship challenge is to insert key audio-visual material as one featured segment of your speech—creating a "show" within your speech, especially to portray a crucial main point. The idea is to keep the overall context and primary flow of the speech "in person," and draw on the power of images only when necessary. Consider the following example.

One CEO included a show of slides in speaking in-person to a major service club about "certification" of forestry and forest-products management on privately owned forest lands. He wanted to explain the value of an industry systematic approach to growing, monitoring, tracing, harvesting, and labeling timber, as well as creating wood and pulp-related manufactured products, all in accord with widely accepted standards.

The speaker began the remarks with a greeting and a compliment to the group regarding one of their successful community-service projects he had learned about. Then he raised the rhetorical question "Do you think we have more or fewer forests today in our country than we did 100 years ago?"

Giving the correct answer as "more," he led into what it takes to develop and maintain—keeping sustainable—timberland holdings for business purposes today and well into the future. His objective in speaking was to uphold what he was convinced are responsible industry standards even though they differ from an independent, non-profit organizations' conservation standards. The relationship between the two programs was quite contentious at the time, and perhaps for many still is today.

After the speaker commented on the two programs overall, he turned head-on into a key issue of the day, "clearcutting," presenting slides that combined maps, images, and photos from a variety of sources. These included a museum of natural history,[1] the client company's library of materials and historical files, and material from a larger forest products company.

The Backstory

As the lights came down and the slides went up, the audience seemed fascinated in discovering how trees developed over the millennia. Many people—if not the majority—assume there originally was a "pristine sea of green" in forest lands until people moved in and "destroyed" the environment.

Such an immaculate sea of green never was the case.

The slides showed how much of the Pacific Northwest once was covered with an extensive ice sheet long (actually 16,000 years) ago. As the climate changed, the ice sheet began to melt and pull back to the north, exposing land ripe for new growth. Trees began to appear here and there, and people started to move in—at about the same time. In fact, trees and people grew up together. Along with this, fire, windstorms, and pestilence took their toll on the forestlands. Trees grew in a scarred patchwork throughout the area. At first, humankind's influence was not particularly noticeable or significant.

As conditions continued to change and populations grew, people started to take the upper hand, cutting down more and more trees, using harvest practices that began to threaten the future of key forestlands. Conservationists and forest products companies began to wrestle with how to protect trees, the forest environment, and business investments for the future.

The speaker explained that the resulting goal for conservationists as well as many landowners in the forest products business today is to "certify" programs to safeguard forests and assure good forestry.

One outcome is the environmentalist-endorsed "Forest Stewardship Council" set of practices; the other is the industry-endorsed "Sustainable Forestry Initiative." Both sets of standards deal especially with the controversial practice of clearcutting.

The Effects

In addressing clearcutting head-on, the speaker showed how old-growth trees were cut more than 100 years ago in the heart of the city of Vancouver, B.C. "In the area known as Pacific Spirit Park [in Vancouver] today," he said, "all the trees were cut away, and nothing was replanted— practices that are long out-of-date."

The speaker pointed out that left to recover on their own, "the trees in the park grew back into a hearty stand that today looks just like a natural rainforest." He said, "Forests are very capable of self-renewal."

In regard to clearcutting on privately owned lands, he raised the question, "How can we manage clearcutting's one particularly big problem? Clearcutting looks bad," he said. "Unfortunately, to some people, if something looks bad it must be bad."

Clearcutting and Sustainability

Using slides, the speaker went on to show his perspective on the tradeoffs among selective harvesting, natural recovery from clearcutting, and clearcutting coupled with modern sustainable tree-farming practices.

He pointed out how "selective cutting" means seedlings have to grow in shade and competition with full-grown trees. Regarding clearcutting today, he showed the industry standards companies like his followed, including the use of computer modeling to maximize aesthetics. Then he showed evident benefits of a modern approach to regenerating the forest.

"For many tree species, particularly Douglas fir and redwood," he said, "clearcutting usually is the harvesting method that best provides the environment necessary for prompt regeneration and rapid re-growth of the forest. These species require full sunlight for seedling or sprout development ... and grow best when exposed fully to the sun." "A redwood or Douglas fir grown in an area that was clear-cut will be much larger," he said, "than one of the same age that has been shaded beneath a canopy of larger trees."

Coup de Gras

It helps in covering a topic like this to introduce an element of drama, especially a striking visual.

As evidence, he showed a slide of localized forest recovery after the well-known eruption of Mt. St. Helens in Washington state in 1980.

At a boundary line, on one side blatantly evident were benefits of the tree-farming methods used by the largest company in the region. On the other side of the boundary were the results of "natural" recovery, the government side of the boundary.

The healthy, vibrant young trees on the company's farmed side were amazing as compared with the immature starts on the natural, government side. No abundance of "best words" could have portrayed the difference as effectively as this photo did.

As the lights went back up, the speaker turned off the slides, engaged the audience once again eye to eye, and proceeded to finish his speech. He went on to cover his third main point, then a summary, and the conclusion, followed by Q&A.

You may not agree with some of his thoughts and conclusions. This author witnessed his sincerity and good intentions, and appreciated his willingness to speak to community audiences.

Toward the end of the series of such speeches he reached out to engage with a major conservation-minded constituency. They welcomed his speech. We showed up, but no one else attended. While the notion of outreach is great, sometimes it doesn't always work. The client persevered with other speeches, nonetheless, and in the process became an excellent speaker, with feedback data to prove it.

The point of this example most especially is the importance, when including a slide segment in your speech, of (1) establishing a good connection with the audience in the early segments of your speech (introduction, theme, first main point), (2) then perhaps as a second main point, introducing your visuals to nail your message, and (3) then coming back face-to-face to finish your remarks in person, including the summary and the conclusion.

As long as your talk doesn't just become a slide or video show, judicious use of visuals can help make your remarks lively. Even so, make a point of ending on a note of personal engagement.

Manage Technical Logistics Carefully

It's likely you've seen other top executives try to manage their own in-person projection equipment on-site—and do a terrible job. Many executives speaking in-person fumble with their laptop and visuals right up to the last minute, missing the opportunity to meet and greet members of the audience. Some speakers cut off Q&A time to take down their equipment and run to their next appointment, finishing on what can be seen as a sour note. You can do better than this.

If you feel particularly challenged, it pays to have a savvy technician with you on the spot to make things right. If you can't, perhaps it's best to forego the visuals.

A (Somewhat) Good Morning

A different twist on the use of visuals was a client's intention to show a video during the opening segment of an in-person keynote speech at a major industry conference. His speech was intended to kick off a technical operations conference first thing in the morning. In his job as the new head of national-level retail operations he was implementing the use of Six Sigma performance standards nationwide. His subject was "Six Sigma" quality-improvement methods.

The challenge was to develop a beginning that would be an eye opener, quickly show how his company was adopting new technical standards, and conclude with selling the benefits the speaker was promoting.

Fortunately, one of this company's large customers was a nationally recognized fast-food retailer with extensive breakfast-treat operations, and had incorporated Six Sigma principles throughout its stores. For the speech, we worked with the client's staff, his top retail managers, and the customer's leadership to produce a lively video of the new technical practices in action. The idea was to present a visual "breakfast treat" meant to wake up the audience.

Alas, the speaker was taken ill in getting to the conference, and at the last minute was unable to bring the video with him into the conference center.

And yet, because he had done his homework and knew his material, he still was able to explain the Six Sigma example well enough to make his main points clear and convincing. A visual breakfast was not served, but his remarks—and the coffee served at the break afterwards—were much appreciated. Follow-up conversations were lively, and in the end the feedback was good.

Most likely you indeed can put together lively visual material that can make your day, and do very well with it. That's the major point of this chapter.

A useful lesson, though, is that even when you prepare visuals to be a slick and professional "show" within your speech, be ready to go it alone if something goes wrong. If that happens, you still can save the day if you're well prepared.

CHAPTER 19

Be Flexible

So far we've considered speech structure, perspectives on addressing community audiences online and in-person, research about co-questioning and empathetic outreach, dealing with audience thoughts and feelings, storytelling, outlining and drafting your remarks, using smooth transitions, and adding special touches including visuals to make your speech effective and memorable.

So what's a good way to open the door to effectiveness at the forum as you begin, even before you start speaking?

Connecting with the Audience

For an in-person speech, one way to optimize your performance is to arrive early enough to greet a few people as they enter, and actually have a conversation with at least two or three of them. Then, as you begin your speech, make a point of acknowledging these audience members at least briefly.

For an online speech, as you begin you could mention something you've learned that the group is doing or aspires to do, especially if you have that interest in common. At a remote site, you could comment on something in the local news or that your team is involved in to show that you're interested in what's happening in the community. A different approach would be to comment on the group's good reputation and why you especially were looking forward to joining them this day.

The point is to put them first at least to some extent if possible.

Prepare for the Unexpected

Let's reflect a little further on preparing—for the unexpected! Circumstances can be quite unpredictable.

Perhaps your introducer or host will skip key points that could help the audience tune into who you are. Maybe you'll follow a tough act, or there could be a much more popular speaker on an especially timely topic coming up next on the program. On the other hand, the audience may be eager to get on with a ceremony of some sort after you're done, or looking forward to some special entertainment.

Even more challenging, what if just before you're up to speak you are feeling out of sorts or having an "off day"? And what if your host flubs the introduction? What should you do?

Help the Introducer, Get Going

For starters, if the introducer skips a key point that leads into your speech, be prepared to add the point succinctly and discreetly as you thank the person and begin your speech. Don't dawdle. Once you get going you'll be fine.

What if you sense your speech is beginning to drag, or if your audience gets distracted in some way at some point? Prepare for this in advance with a rhetorical question or two that you could ask in order to reconnect with your listeners and go further into your material.

After a meal, the audience's circadian rhythms may make them a bit sleepy. In this case add a brief story you've prepared, perhaps a self-deprecating, humorous story leading into your material. Such a touch can inspire closer attention, establish your line of thought engagingly, and help you and your audience ultimately finish your speech at the same time—always a good thing.

You also could prepare an alternative main point that's a bit livelier. Or you could add a quick list—an "A, B, and C" of this, or a "top ten" of that. In any case, develop at least one good alternative in advance in case you need one.

They're on Your Side

Remember that the audience overall wants you to succeed, they're on your side! They may not care about you personally all that much, but they do want to feel good about being there and the time they're spending, likely with their friends, listening to you.

If you prepare well, and make a point to engage with them, they'll be able to tell you care. They'll appreciate your efforts, and they'll pay attention.

CHAPTER 20

In Good Humor—
Further Examples

It's no secret that many of us, despite all the good advice to the contrary, in preparing a speech spend a fair share of time looking through joke books and humor columns, watching late-night comedians, and searching the Internet for wit, inspiration and whimsy to use in a speech.

A Comedian?

No one expects an executive to be a comedian. Sure, a good and relevant joke can be fun, and you may have a gift for humor to some extent. Sometimes you may actually be entertaining.

But your audiences want to hear about what you know and are good at, and how it could affect or help them. So don't waste time trying too hard to start with a joke, especially if you're not really that funny.

A Joke on You

If you can't help trying some humor, you could tell your listeners about a time when the joke was on you—self-deprecating humor. Ideally, the humor would support a key message in your speech. Or maybe you could tell a story about a relevant mistake you made and learned from (humility works well), or a funny misunderstanding you eventually figured out how to unravel.

Disbelief?

Do you believe you've never had something funny, memorable, or at least notable happen to you? This excuse is more common among business people than you might think. If you talk this over with someone who knows you well, however, they may suggest something noteworthy about you, or something funny enough you've done or experienced that could be useable in a speech.

In addition, each of us has learned something from awkward experiences or flat-out mistakes that in hindsight are funny, and—if you choose wisely what to say and explain the situation clearly—such an anecdote can help you prove a point and enhance your credibility.

Try a Joke—Maybe

To every rule there may be exceptions. If you know you can tell a joke reasonably well, and people who know you agree, you might experiment with a truly relevant joke to start your speech. Test out your material with a friend. Keep it short—quickly get to the punch line. Practice. You may have a winner!

A touch of humor is especially appropriate at a dinner or an upbeat ceremonial event, when everyone is a little more relaxed and looking to have a good time—if the occasion reasonably allows some humor. Above all, never try "standup," telling a series of jokes. That's a recipe for disaster. Leave that to the professionals. Play it safe, for the sake of your audience, your customers, your investors, your associates, and your career.

CHAPTER 21

Be True to Your "Voice"

Let's focus on what should be a "big picture" item in preparing your speech: your "voice," your natural style of speaking. In a discussion about this with a senior corporate communications manager, she noted some tips that could help:

- For writing in conversational style, read your material out loud, even make a recording for yourself and play it back perhaps more than once.
- Strive for an overall speech-content pattern that sounds like you, jibes with how you naturally tend to think.
- Use examples and stories that come from your recent experiences.
- Make references occasionally to major sources that you tend to follow (for example, industry leaders, other top executives, analysts, social media feeds, industry journals, columnists, thought-leading commentaries, researchers, and public opinion polls).
- Express a consistent feeling of regard for the audience.
- Present a tone of sensitivity, courtesy, and/or frankness that is characteristic of you—but don't fake it.
- Be comfortable with a level of stature that suits you—not too high, not too low.

If that manager reviewed this list today, she characteristically would say, "Do all of these things!"

First Steps

To capture one speaker's personal voice, what helped this writer was the speaker's habit of earmarking articles he found interesting and thought-provoking, and putting them into a special file that was easy for me to access. When we met to begin working on an upcoming speech, we'd discuss useful points from those articles.

In meeting with a client, this speechwriter focused not only on thoughts and stories but also the person's choice of words, ways of raising questions and evaluating a topic, especially on points that might be of interest to the audience. Our back-and-forth exchanges sharpened our mutual understanding, helped this writer "get" the speaker's views and patterns of expression, and helped us nail key thoughts.

Uncovering Those Personal Stories

For authenticity, as noted previously, a personal story or two in a speech can make all the difference. If you are writing for someone else, be on the lookout for unique stories that might come up in your meetings or conversations, and in speech rehearsals. Associates and friends also may have good suggestions.

One client believed she really didn't have interesting stories to tell about herself. So we considered stories about people that she admired—inspiring personalities in the news, business leaders, bosses, teachers, and memorable peers, staff members who she felt deserved special recognition, and sometimes customers if customer confidentiality could be maintained. This did not and should not include naming names, of course, unless you get permission or the story is about a public figure (even then, be careful). Often, she referred to a widely-known corporate chief who mentored her early in her career.

Such stories say a lot about you, of course—ideals, life-changing experiences, your character. And they add color, respect, emotion, humor, and personality. The audience will accept and like such stories readily if they are relevant and real.

Writing for the Ear

Another major part of the equation for a speaker to sound authentic is to make sure written material is drafted carefully for the ear. In general, this of course means making it conversational.

To add to what was mentioned in previous chapters about this, conversational material means short sentences and everyday words, contractions, and a variety of pauses, some shorter and some longer. Add to that a few of your favorite expressions, especially terms that people who know you would recognize as characteristic, familiar, and natural. Intermittently this writer would mark "pause" in a script, for a key idea to sink in, for a break, or as a transition.

In rehearsal, if something written is out of tune, artificial, you'll stumble or feel uncomfortable with it, and it'll be obvious that a script adjustment is needed. Make it.

All this takes work, some humility, and patience, but in the end will make your remarks more enjoyable, and convincing.

CHAPTER 22

The End (of Your Speech)

So far, we've discussed techniques for researching and writing your speech. Let's cut to "The End"—how to close. Consider three possibilities: the classic close, what not to do, and some variations you could try.

Classic Close

The classic close steps logically from the introduction, theme, major points, and a summary. The conclusion should be a call to action, an "ask":

- To try something new.
- To avoid something (such as a misleading source of information).
- To weigh the pros and cons of an issue that's evolving day by day.
- Or simply to reflect on the theme of your talk.

You may be able to end with a combination of these points.

What Not to Do

Even seasoned teachers of speech composition may forget to say this: do not end with "thanking" your audience. A meekly delivered "thank you" intended to be humble and not too self-serving does not work. Don't weaken your talk by leaving the audience with the impression that you aren't too sure of yourself and what you just said.

Despite your best intentions and intended humility, saying thank you at this point cheapens your message. Make your final point firmly, and stop. If you've done your job, the audience will feel like thanking YOU! They will do so if you give them the opportunity.

If you can't keep yourself from being thankful (perhaps the real reason is that you are especially thankful that you are done!), then you at least could thank the presider for inviting you to speak. Even so, it's much better simply to trust yourself that you can carry the day, and end on a strong note leading to applause, or at least to evident thankfulness by the audience.

If you do the work prescribed in our previous chapters, your audience indeed will *want* to thank you—and will do so spontaneously.

Variations on "The End"

Like almost anything in the art of public speaking, variations on how to end a speech are innumerable. If time allows after your summary, you could end with an additional, concluding section (as in a music "coda"). For example, you could indicate key action points that follow from the logic of your speech. One client agreed to include five action points in a closing statement; it was strong, dynamic, impressive.

In your speech, one good possibility could be to push for actions that easily could be tracked and reported later as results.

Just don't make your close too complicated.

In General

Usually, good speechwriting means arranging your material so that the ending is simple, one sentence, clearly follows your major points, and makes a strong call to action, at least for the audience to ponder what you are advocating.

CHAPTER 23

Wisdom of the Ages

The material in this chapter at first glance may seem to be outdated and irrelevant. You might be tempted to bypass all this and "get on with it." But don't. There are key points tied to each classic source that are practical and could make a big difference for you.

Advice that was golden two millennia ago still can make your day. Leaders have been struggling for a long time with how to optimize public speaking. Why not consider recommendations straight from the classics that can be right on the money for you today?

Some of the points that follow are elements we've touched on in earlier chapters, but many are new. Let's put it all together, and consider what particularly could be helpful.

First up, heralded in previous chapters as "The Father of Rhetoric," is Aristotle (384 to 322 BC). Then we'll take a brief look at the legendary Roman orator and public figure Cicero (106 BC to 43 BC). Finally, we'll seek some advice from the Chinese philosopher, politician and teacher Confucius (551 to 479 BC). His thoughts suggest an application today to speeches to international audiences.

Aristotle on Persuasion

Aristotle's classic treatise *Rhetoric* was published in 350 BC. It consists of an extended introductory outline, and three "Books," each with several brief chapters. Although his focus was persuasion, law-courts-related and political, his teachings form a solid core that is largely relevant to corporate and organizational speeches today.

In Book One Aristotle says rhetoric—public speaking—"can plainly be handled systematically."[1] In our previous chapters we have already taken a systematic, structural approach, following that advice. Aristotle goes on to identify several crucial points:

100

- "Rhetoric may be defined as the faculty of observing in any given case the available means of persuasion."[2]
- He specifies three kinds of persuasion: (1) the speaker's power of demonstrating a personal character which will make the speech credible, (2) the power of stirring the emotions of the hearers, (3) the power of proving a truth or apparent truth by means of persuasive arguments.[3] In this book our focus is on engagement, not persuasion, but we do want to be credible.
- In regard to character, Aristotle says a speaker should demonstrate "prudence, virtue, and goodwill."[4]
- In discussing emotions, Aristotle advises stirring the emotions of the hearers, and discusses: (1) calmness (as the opposite of anger), (2) friendship and enmity (being opposed, angry, hostile), (3) fear and confidence, (4) shame and shamelessness, (5) kindness and unkindness, (6) pity, (7) indignation, (8) envy, (9) and emulation.[5]

Aristotle considers various patterns of thought including: (1) induction or the use of examples, (2) deduction, and (3) amplification, such as pointing out someone's virtues or "noble" traits in a memorial speech.

Cicero's Five Elements of Public Speaking

Another classic source on public speaking, although still persuasion-oriented, is the famed Roman orator Marcus Tullius Cicero. He was a statesman, lawyer, philosopher, and master of rhetoric. He played a prominent role in upholding the traditions of the Roman Republic. Perhaps his most well-known speeches (at least among students of classic Latin) are his four "Orations Against Cataline," an adamant conspirator. Overall, Cicero's writings include treatises on rhetoric, philosophy, and politics. Especially pertinent here is his analysis of "the material of the art of rhetoric."[6] He emphasized:

- Invention: "The discovery of valid or seemingly valid arguments to render one's cause plausible"—identifying your arguments. (Note: make sure yours are valid!)
- Arrangement: "The distribution of arguments ... in the proper order."
- Expression: "The fitting of the proper language to the invented matter"—careful choice of words, sentence structure, tone, figures of speech, proper emphasis.
- Memory: A "firm mental grasp of matter and words"—in our case, memorizing at least the structure of your speech and key words and expressions.

- Delivery: "The control of voice and body in a manner suitable to the dignity of the subject matter and the style"—your stance, use of a lectern, eye contact, gestures, pronunciation, emphasis, and other patterns of engagement with the audience.

Incidentally, Cicero especially admired the speeches of the classic orators of ancient Athens, particularly Demosthenes. Cicero's own career, influence and demise are as colorful as one could imagine. His politics led to his being beheaded by order of his political rival, Mark Antony, who put Cicero's head and hands on display in the Roman Forum. Beware of politics!

By Memory?

Let's drill down further on Cicero's thoughts about memory and consider some advice dealt with to some extent in our previous chapters. While classic orators like Cicero delivered speeches from memory, today's executive public speaker—unless you have special ability—typically does not have the time or the patience to memorize an entire 17- to 18-minute business speech.

Seldom would this be necessary:

- If your speech is well constructed. It's relatively easy to speak from notes and maintain adequate eye contact if the speech is logical and strongly expressive to begin with.
- If you take the time to internalize the fundamental approach, structure, and style of the speech, including key words and expressions.
- If for an in-person talk you rehearse the speech out loud at least three times, once or twice in front of a willing, if not also well-trained listener, and at least once on-camera so you can see and hear yourself on video.
- If you mark your notes with cues for eye contact, pauses, stage directions, and indications of expression (such as to "smile"), perhaps to vary your voice level, and to gesture at key points.
- If for an online speech you rehearse on-camera all three times, paying attention to details about: (1) your appearance, (2) your use of notes, and (3) your performance overall including eye contact with the camera.
- If you try to memorize the opening of your speech, as well as the summary and conclusion. Any work to do so will boost the effectiveness of your remarks.

Confucius on Communication

For overall discretion and thoughts about speaking to a mixed-language or international audience, let's consider two points from the "Analects" of Confucius. The Analects is an ancient compendium of sayings and ideas attributed to Confucius and his contemporaries, traditionally believed to have been compiled and written by his followers in 475–221 BC.[7]

First is a reminder about overall caution: "From the point of view of speech communication," the Analects said, "do not say anything that you are not sure about, [and] be cautious even when talking about what you generally know. Only in this way can we make fewer mistakes."[8] Today, a careless assertion or an off-the-cuff remark can go viral and come back to haunt you later—not only in an online speech that easily could end up on social media, but also during an in-person speech. Someone might make a video of it.

A second point—especially for an audience you are unfamiliar with— is Confucius' advice to be careful not to speak above (or below) the level of your audience. For most business or organization speeches, you may be speaking to peers or at least people with general business knowledge, but be careful with a less business-oriented audience. Address them in terms that work for them.

Pace of Speaking

Also, in regard to the level of an audience, be careful about how conversant your audience is in the language you are using. When speaking to a non-native-English-speaking audience, especially if you tend to be fast-paced, speak a bit more slowly so that your listeners are able to follow you comfortably.

For example, regarding a client CEO's speech to a group of international business leaders in business-administration training at a major university, the program coordinator asked ahead of time that the speaker be sure to talk somewhat slowly, deliberately—because some students had been uncomfortable in the past with guests who spoke too quickly and were difficult to follow.

If you get into a similar situation, you may need to adjust your pace. Don't demean your audience by speaking too slowly, but don't lose them either. At least talk about this with your host in advance.

If you are quite conversant in a second language, such as Spanish or Mandarin, German or French, be careful to speak clearly and perhaps a bit slowly in that language to a native audience. You could be difficult to understand because of your accent.

As a non-native student in Austria listening to university lectures given in German by a Dutch native, this listener found his accent made him very difficult to understand. Similarly, American colleagues in an outstanding Belgium university, even in a fourth and final year of study, still had a hard time understanding lectures given in French by professors who were not native French speakers.

CHAPTER 24

Anatomy of a Speech

A memorable in-person CEO speech some time ago was very well received—"perfect," according to the forum's presider, who had invited the speaker to begin with. Credit was due not only to the character and wisdom of the speaker, but also the forum's program committee. They agreed that our suggestion for a speech on policies of the Federal Reserve System could be suitable, particularly because "the Fed" controls interest rates—at the time a major concern.

Still, a speech about the Fed might not be too entertaining, not a great way to spend a lunch hour. It was a challenge.

The turnout for the luncheon was some 250–300, quite good. The speaker gave it his best. Surprisingly, after the speech, several audience members even asked for copies of the speech! (Highly unusual, the presider noted.)

Let's take a look at how the speech tied together elements recommended in our preceding chapters, and how teamwork and a seasoned top executive made it work.

Advance Planning

The audience was a forum in a city seen by local and regional management, and headquarters, as a priority market. Local management wanted to show how the company's executives were connected with Federal Reserve System policymakers at the highest level.

In the way the speech was put together by this writer working closely with the local team, after a few calls for background information, the components seemed to work especially well in terms of structure, strategy, and personal touches.

Structure

In fitting the group's 20-minute time limit, the script began with an opening that tied into the introducer's comments (arranged with him in advance), then presented a theme statement, followed by four major points. The theme, with reference to current headlines in the news, acknowledged that the Federal Reserve is generally not well understood, yet affects everyone virtually every day.

In addition to a normal three major points of explanation, a fourth elaborated somewhat on the company's position on a timely aspect of all this. As a business speech, the point was to position the company favorably in the public eye regarding what was happening.

Finally, there was a conclusion that quickly summed up the message, restated the importance of the subject matter, "which affects the future prosperity of each and every one of us," and invited questions.

The structure and the writing carried the speaker's straightforward character, his "voice" (sounding much like a normal conversation), as well as timely points of interest, and had a pleasing flow to it.

Strategy

Some elements worked particularly well because they were sincere—including some unscripted comments that were heart-warming. In the opening, the speaker acknowledged that the introducer, just retired, had been a formidable competitor and someone the speaker had long admired. In such a forum it can make sense to say good things about the competition. Above all, this CEO made a point to speak about his *industry* rather than touting his own company. This helped him catch and hold the attention of the audience throughout the speech.

At that time a lot of people hated the banking industry and the hardships it represented for many. Fortunately, the speaker's bank was well-managed, and continued to be healthy and strong, providing fair and reliable service—and reassurance—in hard times. This CEO could stand forward credibly as a sentinel of strength, truth, and reliability. And he did so.

Approach

In preparing this speech, the "co-questioning" approach included identifying and asking key individuals in advance what pointed questions they might ask the speaker—if they "could just sit down and have a conversation with him for a few minutes," one on one. The research identified the strategic importance of spelling out the company's commitment to the community, and what this could mean in some particular regards.

Also strategic was to reduce the audience's anxieties, dispelling some erroneous preconceptions, about the effects of the industry on the cost of living, as well as the costs of business expansion and growth at the time.

Finally, on a personal, empathetic level, the speaker wanted to note his rural upbringing and his comfort with the community's home-town environment (comments added by the speaker himself). The audience could sense his down-to-earth character, and his open and honest manner. And they felt how he liked the city and the community in general. They appreciated the way he related to them as equals instead of as an aloof out-of-towner.

Personal Touches

The personal elements noted above are classic. As Aristotle said, "It is not true, as some writers assume in their treatises on rhetoric, that the personal goodness revealed by the speaker contributes nothing to the power of persuasion; on the contrary, character may almost be called the most effective means of persuasion one possesses."[1]

This speaker didn't tell jokes, but instead happened to mention his personal feelings about the coming baseball season, his early career aspirations as a pitcher, and his continued love for baseball.

During the speech he also commented briefly about national public figures in the news—individuals he knew personally. His candid yet appropriate insights about industry and political leaders at the national level were surprising, down to earth, impressive, and timely.

On the local business side of the equation, the speaker acknowledged key members from his local management team who were present. He also spoke highly of a professional in the audience who headed up the local office of a related-industry firm for which the speaker was a director. The speaker knew this individual was an active member of the group the speaker was addressing, and had a strong reputation not only in the organization but also the community in general.

This speech became a total win for everyone involved when the speaker noted that he felt "at home" in this community: "I like being here. Perhaps it's my small town, agrarian background that allows me to relate to your city. Regardless of the reason, it seems a wholesome place to live. It's an honor to be here with you today." His sincerity heightened the respect and mutual enjoyment that characterized the talk.

The Net Result

The speech got top reviews among audience members interviewed for feedback afterwards. The speaker touched all the right bases—the company's local manager was quite pleased. Overall, the speech helped put the bank's local team on the high road to good service and further business success in that community.

Some Crucial Dos and Don'ts

Let's summarize some key points from this example. Sure, your situation today may be quite different, but keep these basics in mind, most of which we've advocated in previous chapters:

- Before you agree to give a speech to a public group, be sure to check it out with your local team if you have one there.
- Research the group in some detail, as well as local community issues and sensitivities, the local economy, demographics, perceptions of your industry—and especially local perceptions of your organization, including available public opinion data and recent news coverage, if you have access to such.
- After thanking the introducer, quickly make your opening more about "them"—your audience and something they care about—than about you.
- It's good to discuss your industry rather than just your enterprise, only occasionally giving examples about your business. Honor others in your industry, if that fits. A sales pitch from start to finish about your organization will turn people off.
- Engage with your audience, whether by a "shout out" to an acquaintance who's there, or referring to something current on the local scene.
- Be aware of the audience's feelings. It can be good to express positive feelings you have about the group, the community, the region. If you enjoy being with this particular group, say so.
- Tell a story or two, at least a brief mention of something down-to-earth, perhaps heartwarming about friends or family, or a personal off-the-job interest that people could easily relate to, something memorable.
- Leave time for Q&A; pay special attention to topics people ask about, and follow up with inquisitive individuals later if appropriate.

For an in-person speech like this, take time to meet attendees right before and after the speech. Thank them for their interest in you, your topic, your business. Provide a way to be contacted if they would like to follow up with you (again, bring a one-page handout with basic information about your enterprise—not too "salesy"—including how best to contact you). If it seems proper, offer to contact them, but do so only if you honestly can and will make the effort to follow up.

In this particular case, after his talk the speaker made himself available for media interviews, and arranged with his local team to meet with selected customers and prospects. Take advantage of such business opportunities if and when you can!

Speech Delivery

CHAPTER 25

Be Well Introduced

Your public speaking will be more effective if you help your introducer, the audience, and yourself get off to a good start. Give your introducer useful material to work with. Just sending a bio is not enough. You could offer a draft introduction that covers relevant points, and suggest the introducer should feel free to personalize what you provide.

This may be much more important than you realize, for several reasons. How you are introduced—unless you are a well-known public figure—is a great opportunity to demonstrate your experience, your character, and establish credibility even before you greet your audience. Secondly, this avoids having an introducer ramble through a bio-sheet or a resume, wasting precious time for you not only to speak but also to take questions from the audience at the end.

In addition, how you are introduced will clarify what your talk will be all about, get their attention, and can put the audience in a receptive frame of mind. So take full advantage of the opportunity and give the introducer good, brief, relevant material to use in opening the door for you to give an effective speech.

Accordingly, if you're an introducer, seek introductory material from the speaker well in advance, even review with the speaker what you intend to say. Experienced speakers will appreciate your efforts to help them do well, and so, albeit indirectly, will your audience.

Introductory Structure

The good introduction should include a simple beginning, and possibly two more (very brief) major points.

The beginning should state the name of the speaker, and the title or general topic of the speech. The second major point of an introduction likely should address a few bio details and a speaker's industry experience.

A third main point could be a comment about special expertise the speaker has regarding the subject of the speech, or why the topic is especially timely. This could go on briefly to include special community-involvement initiatives the speaker or the enterprise is involved in currently.

Finally, the end of the introduction should restate the name of the speaker and the topic or title of the speech, and lead into welcoming applause if appropriate (not for an online talk, of course). Such a restatement will help anyone who was not able to hear the beginning, wasn't paying attention, just walked into the room, or was late (there usually are a couple of late arrivals, whatever the occasion).

Timing

In general, the introduction usually should take only a minute or two. On average, in my experience, speakers talk at approximately 110 words per minute, so the total number of words in the introduction should be set accordingly.

To sum up, a good introduction carefully frames the subject, the speaker, and quickly gets the speaker off to an energized start.

A Redacted Example:

Our guest speaker today is (full name), the Chairman, President & Chief Executive Officer of _____ (bank). His/her topic is the effects of _____ regulations on homebuyers and community businesses.

_____ is the largest bank headquartered in _____, managing $_____ in assets and _____ branches located in _____ western states.

_____ joined the bank in _____. His/her prior positions included work with _____. He/she started his/her career with _____ in _____.

(First name) also is a former Director of the _____, a former Chairman of the _____ of the _____ Association, and serves on the boards of _____ and civic groups including _____ as well as _____.

He/she holds a _____ degree in _____ from the University of _____, and is a graduate of the _____ Graduate School of _____ at _____.

Please join me in welcoming ... (full name) _____ (lead the applause!).

CHAPTER 26

Co-Focus Your Opening

A friend once commented, "If the speaker doesn't catch me in the first minute, I stop listening."

Why is such stopping often the case? What could a speaker do to get off to a better start? Overall, your opening could include a special element to co-focus[1] your remarks—catch and connect with your audience. Consider the following suggestions.

In thanking the introducer, make a brief, positive comment about the occasion, or about something the audience may already have in mind, such as a project members of the group are engaged in. Maybe there's something special being celebrated or commemorated that day. Perhaps something relevant came up in the preliminaries before you were introduced, such as a major announcement, or a special event or outreach project the group is preparing for.

Based on your preliminary research, perhaps you could share something positive that impressed you about the group and its role in the local community. Maybe there's something in the news of the day that relates to your topic. Is there a particular reason why you've looked forward to this occasion?

Ideally, be prepared to focus briefly on something that relates your subject matter to the audience, perhaps about your overall theme or one of your main points.

Prepare, Be Flexible

When you rehearse your material, think about options for the opening. Consider a couple of options. Have you already picked up on something special that connects you and your message with the audience?

When the time comes, be ready to give them a hearty, "verbal handshake" at the outset and quickly get off to a good start.

Small point? Makes a big difference.

CHAPTER 27

Techniques for Good
In-Person Delivery

We've considered classic principles, innovative strategy, creativity, and good writing. Let's turn to some finer points about speech delivery—it's crucial.

Your Script

Be strict with yourself about timing. As pointed out already, an invitation for "a 20-minute in-person speech plus time for questions" typically means no more than 17–18 minutes of rehearsed script. For virtual talks you may be asked to speak for a shorter time, perhaps 15 minutes. In either case leave enough Q&A time for the audience, which could provide great value to everyone, yourself included. Event programs often run late, and introducers usually take too long, so Q&A time often gets cut short.

Your actual delivery time often will be at least a minute or two longer than you expect, no matter how many times you practice. This seems to happen especially at breakfast and luncheon events, so edit accordingly. If you don't, when the scheduled time is up, the audience may "depart," walk out the door—at least in terms of their attention—even if you are still speaking.

For ease of delivery, make sure your script, if you use one, is word processed to print only on the top two-thirds of the page—so you are not reading down into the very bottom of the page, pulling your head down too far, leaving the audience wondering where you "went."

Most often, even today, a printed script still is best. Large type for the script is good—16 pt. Times New Roman, a serif typeface (easier to read), is ideal. All of this makes it easier for you to keep good eye contact with the audience.

If you choose to read from a laptop screen (usually awkward and may be unpredictable), set it up high enough to help you keep eye contact with your audience as much as possible.

If you want or are directed to use a teleprompter, rehearse with the full setup a couple of times so you are comfortable when you go "live."

Stage Directions for an In-Person Speech

It helps to make marginal (side) notes on your script, including stage directions for yourself—where to stand, when to move, where to look, to pick up your pace. You could add a note or two in the margin to check the time at key points so you can keep from running too long. You might even want to use a silent timer to alert you when your time is about up.

Eye Contact

For in-person speech delivery, pick out three individuals to address, to have a "conversation" with "meaningfully" during your speech. Do not just look up routinely as you go, with quick, impersonal glances. Linger for a moment, engage a bit, vary your focus.

Be aware of any tendency to speak to one side most of the time. (This author recently attended a major presentation by a university executive, who stood to one side of the stage to start with, and talked the whole time just to a small cluster of listeners right in front of him. Beyond annoying!)

Right-handers tend to look to the right, and left-handers to the left. Try to balance your eye contact. Keep in mind that you are trying to build a connection with your listeners. Be interested in how they are doing, and how they are reacting.

Further Techniques

To keep organized (for either an in-person talk or an online session) consider getting a Script-Master™[1] or a similar professional-looking, efficient script holder. Even just a plain, thin, black notebook for your notes can work, if you can keep them from falling out. Set up your script so you can slide pages to the side rather than flipping them over, which can create mic noise, distract the audience, or both.

Keep your notes in order. After the speech, you may be asked by someone—in a media interview, or by a member of the audience, perhaps a prospective customer—to repeat an element of your remarks. An orderly script makes it easier to find the right material quickly.

While delivering your speech, loosen up a bit; perhaps make a marginal note on your script to "relax." Be kind to yourself.

For an in-person speech, remember to keep your mouth the same distance from a stationary lectern mic in order to keep the volume consistent. Even better, use a lavalier mic if possible.

For a virtual speech, it's OK to change positions occasionally, but always keep good eye contact with the camera—the eye of the camera is your sweet spot. If you are seated, do not rock back and forth (an occasional news commentator does this on-camera; it's distracting and annoying). No squirming around.

In any case, have a glass of water on hand, in case you need it. That's standard procedure, for good reason.

Keep Track of Questions

Finally, have someone track questions for you—questions can be gold for you and your staff to mine later. It's likely that the program or event chair would help you with this if you ask in advance.

CHAPTER 28

Eliminate Ums, Uhs, and Ahs

Let's tackle the awful, dogged habit of voicing such annoying fill words—noise—as "ums," "uhs," and "ahs" during a speech. This is a tendency that can sneak into delivery even for a veteran public speaker. Too often a speaker is not even aware of these mistakes, which we could call "verbal pauses."

For that reason, speech-coaching clubs typically appoint an "ah-counter" to draw attention to such behavior, so speakers realize how often they do this, and eradicate such bad habits.

To work on this, you might ask someone to record—even just on a cellphone—at least part of your next speech so you can listen to yourself and see if you're guilty of bad verbal behavior.

Just as your grammar teachers had little patience for dangling modifiers and run-on sentences, your speech audiences will cringe at your annoying ums, ahs, and similar drivel—and turn you off completely if you do this continuously. Yours truly recently witnessed a speaker who had a habit of uttering an upward sigh at the end of many sentences, presumably to add emphasis. Yikes!

It Starts with Awareness

Sometimes when you add filler noises you may feel they are energizing, helping you seem engaged or thoughtful because you are expressing energy as you catch up with your thoughts. Don't kid yourself. The effect is just the opposite, you sound foolish. There's no need to make useless noises. Just stop for a moment, make a silent pause, and then go on. Timing is important, not too short a pause, not too long. Experiment a bit and pay attention to audience reactions to see what works for you.

"There's no need to make useless
noises. Just stop for a moment, make
a silent pause, and then go on."

In any case, relax, it's OK, the audience will be fine, they'll stay with you.

Even just awareness of a tendency to make verbal pauses may be enough to help you break "uh" and "ah" habits—but you'll probably need to work on this for a good while to clean up your act. That's normal, we've all been there. Bad habits are hard to stop. You'll get there.

When you rehearse your speech using video, even just your cell phone, listen to yourself. If you catch yourself making verbalized pauses in particular sections of your talk, give those points extra attention. A little editing might help. You may need to pause somehow because a sentence is too long; if so, shorten it. Perhaps some words are too complicated or daunting in some way; simplify.

Also, if you know you'll especially be tempted to "um" and "ah" at a specific point despite your best intentions, look a few words ahead in your script and mark an upcoming word to emphasize, a strong point to look forward to. Knowing there's a strong foothold ahead could help you keep moving ahead smoothly.

Silent Pauses Can Be Good

Remind yourself, perhaps with a note in the margin of your script— or centered in your text—if you do need to pause, and practice being silent when you do. If you make a quiet pause on purpose—with confidence— your listeners will wait, will consider what you just said, and will be comfortable. They may look forward to such pauses that are well-timed.

A silent pause can be especially useful for helping the audience absorb a key point, letting it sink in for a moment. A good silent pause also can help you wind up a bit to lead into a next main point emphatically. All good—but don't overdo it.

In preparing scripts for clients, when desirable this writer inserts parenthetical instructions to pause, typically after a paragraph, with the notation centered on a new line after the preceding sentence and before the next.

Proactive "Punctuation"

Consider that you can use behavior to punctuate your remarks a bit more dramatically, eliminating noises and adding emphasis, what R.F. Carter calls "positive punctuation."[1] This is a matter of making speech transitions by voice, gesture, and pace—so that you do something constructive or even assertive instead of hemming and hawing. Such positive punctuation could include:

- Adding: stop a moment in order to then add a further thought (do this only occasionally, too much repetition could be annoying).
- Comparing or contrasting: gesture with one hand, then the other (do not overdo this either, once or twice may be sufficient).
- Conceding: step back slightly (obviously, only for an in-person speech, and only with a lavalier mic).
- Diverting or amusing: use a lighter tone of voice to suggest a feeling of "by the way."
- Exemplifying: introduce an example with a different, possibly lighter expression, even (for an in-person speech) changing your position at the lectern or onstage. Audiences appreciate this.
- Generalizing: change your voice volume or speed—louder, slower, or faster.
- Restating: in repeating a key idea, to let it sink in speak a bit more slowly.
- Sequencing: when using a rhetorical question to ask, or at least suggest, what could happen or come next, let the question hang in the air for a moment before you proceed.
- Summarizing: pause a moment, then deliver a direct, matter-of-fact recap.

Pay Attention

If you pay attention to speech delivery, get rid of those dreadful uhs, ums, and ahs, and add some new dynamics with proactive punctuation, your audiences will be grateful, and your public speaking will be much more effective.

CHAPTER 29

Personalize Your Delivery

Experienced speakers typically have learned a few special ways to personalize their delivery, making their speeches memorable and especially effective. Let's consider some examples that could work for you.

"Shout Out"

Give a "shout out" or two during the opening segment to recognize one or two people in the audience you know, or that you met and conversed with shortly before the speech. We've mentioned this in earlier chapters, but it's easy to forget to do so. A personal touch like this helps engage everyone in the audience, and helps you relax and adopt a friendly tone in place of nervous stiffness. A "shout out" or two might even be useful as you go along, especially if you acknowledge a popular individual in the audience who you know would agree with you and readily support what you are saying.

Personal Eye Contact

For an in-person speech, to personalize your eye contact, pick out three individuals in different parts of the room to "have a conversation with" as you speak. Vary your eye contact with them comfortably during your speech, so it's not too personal. For a virtual talk, however, keep looking at the camera, don't try to have eye contact with icons on-screen. That's talking to nobody!

In person, nothing is more personal than well-intentioned contact eye to eye.

Cue Yourself

Set up written cues for yourself on your script for better delivery. We've touched on this already, but it's hard to overdo such cues—so be generous to yourself.

Have you ever noticed that some people have a habitually stern or unfriendly expression on their face, but then you discover that they are really not that way at all? It's easy to fall into habits of off-putting facial expressions. In speaking to community audiences, try to look kind, be kind.

If you suspect you too often look unfriendly, and are lucky to have observant and tactful friends or a good coach, ask them for help in managing your expressions. Otherwise, watch yourself on video to get direct visual feedback. Get a video somehow of at least part of your latest in-person public speech; there's really no excuse for not trying to do so in this era of smart phones. Take a good look at what you see—what could you do better?

Turn weaknesses into strengths. On your next script, mark cues for things to work on. Some examples—for an in-person speech—might be:

- If you tend to look too much to one side of the audience, for example to the right side, make a point to look to the other side for long moments.
- If you tend to "gorilla grip" the lectern, keep your hands totally off of the lectern, or at least place them in the middle, in front of you.
- If you tend to speak on and on at a fast pace, give yourself and the audience break points, and make those notes to pause from time to time.
- If you tend to sway from side to side, stand still. Don't be a juvenile on a swing.
- When using a lavalier mic, if you tend to pace back and forth, make a point instead to move a little to one side briefly, then back to the center, and stop. Then, a bit later, move again to the other side. Mix the patterns throughout the speech so your moves are not predictable and distracting. Match your moves to key points in the script when changing gears like this makes sense.
- If your voice tends to tire, weaken, or get scratchy as you speak, stop and sip some water. Your audience won't mind. You'll feel better.

Rehearse Three Times

For either an online or an in-person speech, after you flesh out your script, as noted earlier in this book, rehearse your talk out loud three times. Edit as you go, to smooth the rough edges and achieve the length that's just right for the occasion.

Rehearse once for overall content. Then a second time to work on transitions and the flow of your thoughts. Finally, a third time to work on delivery specifics, considering eye contact and dynamics mentioned above.

For an in-person talk, work on keeping your weight evenly on both feet, no swaying from side to side. Leave your hands relatively free for making gestures.

For both in-person or online delivery, practice using the microphone (speak across the top, not spitting into it), and using your notes. It may just seem mechanical and not important; it is important.

In-person, for sake of eye contact, consider the layout of the room where you'll be speaking. Sometimes you may be speaking in a room that is wider than it is long, and you'll need to make a point to adjust your eye contact accordingly, connecting with both sides of the room. For a longer room, be sure to look to the back; people in front will still feel like you're looking at them.

If you take the time to rehearse like this, you'll enable yourself to deliver with strong, nicely flowing, personal dynamics, instead of just pushing through a laundry list of "points." That's boring. An audience will sense your dedication and intentions for good delivery, and will better appreciate what you have to say.

Practicing honors your audience, as well as making you and your organization look good, helping you get the results you want.

Leave Time for Questions, Conversation

A question-and-answer session at the end of your speech could be the most memorable and useful segment of your time for any audience member who "dares" to ask a question, for the audience generally, and, again, for you to learn something new. In the spirit of co-questioning you're out to learn something new yourself; it's engaging.

After your speech is over, stay a couple of minutes to take a couple of follow-up questions, or acknowledge someone who wants to meet you, or reach out to someone you've noticed is there and seems particularly interested. Your audience will notice, at least a few will; it's a mark of sincerity.

With such patience, respect, and positive regard, you'll reinforce your efforts to form new relationships and earn your listeners' support.

CHAPTER 30

Q&A Dynamics

Your speech is given, you catch your breath, and it's over—almost! Wait a minute: it's time for "Questions & Answers." Let's take a more in-depth look at this special opportunity. Be sure to handle it carefully.

Take Questions During or After?

Before we go further, let's be clear that in a public address, particularly with a large audience (at least larger than "classroom" size), it's usually best at the outset to ask your audience to hold their questions to the end of your prepared remarks.

For when that time comes, in advance work out Q&A logistics with your introducer, who likely is also the emcee. Decide who will be "in charge" to call for and take questions, one at a time, and agree on who will bring the session to a close.

It could be best for the emcee to take the lead all the way through instead of you. A good emcee can reduce a predominance of questions from individuals known to take charge of a discussion or make lengthy "statements" instead of asking a specific question. The emcee also could look for more reserved individuals who tend to ask especially useful, interesting, and insightful questions.

How to Answer

For your part, the basic dynamics in answering questions call for you to: (1) repeat the question briefly so all can hear it (while giving yourself a moment to reflect), (2) start with a short and direct answer, and (3) if appropriate, elaborate perhaps with a brief example, or a story if there's time.

As you field questions, try to get a sense of a pattern among questions asked, to touch further on an underlying issue or concern if there is one.

If you feel there is a to-the-point question hanging in the air but not yet asked, you could pose it as a rhetorical question yourself, perhaps starting with "You might wonder if...." Then go on to state what your listeners seem to be wondering about, and deal with it.

A Good Q&A Question

So what constitutes a particularly good Q&A question? Is it truly possible to identify basic questions that are "best"? Journalistic training specifies the pointed questions "who, what, when, where, why, and how."

Years as a market researcher, writer, and public speech professional have taught me that "why" usually is the crucial point underneath it all. Even if it's not quite asked by an audience member, when fielding questions be sure to listen carefully, and if the "why" hasn't quite been asked, it might be wise to deal with it directly.

Hearing, appreciating, and responding to questions takes patience, humility, and insight.

Scripting Answers

In preparing to address a key audience, especially when there may be media coverage on a hot topic, you may be fortunate to have a speechwriter or a public relations, marketing, or investor relations professional to depend on. Someone who can help identify in advance key questions that would come up, and prepare succinct answers for you. If that's not in the cards, you at least can build on your initial audience research, and write out some useful answers yourself.

Developing a polished list of answers to sensitive questions is especially important if you know there could be regulatory, financial, and/ or legal matters at stake. You may want to review your answers with an attorney.

In any case, make sure that prepared answers are in your own words as much as possible, so you can sound natural, credible—and don't make any big mistakes.

Thinking on Your Feet

Some of us are good at thinking on our feet, and some of us are not. This is not necessarily a matter of talent. Like most anything else, it's about doing your homework, and putting your mind to it.

Consider three basic thought tools you can use on the spot, tying together key elements via inside-outside, before-after, and/or similarity-difference relationships.[1] Quite useful is the "inside vs. outside" relationship. You could drill down on a key detail responsive to what the questioner is driving at, or maybe you need to acknowledge the bigger picture for what you are saying. A crucial detail or the broader picture could make all the difference in clarifying your point, helping the audience understand what you are trying to say.

Another good tool is the "before vs. after" relationship. You could look back to one or more conditions that have led to the matter at hand. Or it may be crucial to look ahead to consequences you or others foresee. Or perhaps what is needed is an overall sequence of events to portray a big picture you have in mind.

Also useful is the "similarity vs. difference" relationship. You could point out that a problematic situation is like one earlier and how that worked out, or emphasize what is unique about the current situation that requires a new approach, now.

In any case, keep your answers short and direct—watch the time and don't drag out your answers into another "speech."

How Valuable Is the Q&A Period?

A few clients (and teachers) have intimated that their payoff in giving a speech includes getting at least one good question in the Q&A period, something to reflect on later. A useful question can lead to improving a service, a product, or even strengthening the speaker's overall business model.

Welcome questions, and treasure the good ones!

CHAPTER 31

The Unfriendly, Perhaps Hostile Audience

Dealing with the occasional unfriendly, perhaps even hostile, audience takes us into unsure waters—let's go further into this. Typically, an executive or community leader is invited to speak to a hospitable group about a topic of mutual interest. But not always.

High Emotion

A highly respected church leader arranged to speak to a local congregation about a matter that was upsetting to that audience and many others in the community. He came to a special assembly to answer questions and provide assurance. His plan was to ask members of the audience at the outset to write down their questions on note cards, so that he could answer them in an orderly fashion.

The climate was *contentious*, however. As the rather controlling, if not stifling intended process began, some frustrated members of the audience started to object, outright. They started *shouting* their concerns, sometimes with considerable anger! It seemed the speaker had no idea that the audience would be so hostile.

Fortunately, the majority of the audience was civil enough to allow the speaker to change gears and answer these audience members directly, more spontaneously. He quickly opened the forum so everyone could ask any and all questions—and so he could "hear" their concerns. People wanted to be heard, more than anything.

He made it a point to listen carefully, as well as to speak. Many participants were patient, some were upset, a few shouted out their complaints. Unfortunately, too much was wrong and out of control. People simmered down, and things went better. Finally, time ran out. But a lot of the initial written questions went unanswered. In the end, no one was satisfied with what had transpired, the speaker included.

Work on Key Interviews in Advance

What can we learn from this? The issues at hand made it essential for this executive to make an appearance, to talk with the group, and to assure everyone that he was taking appropriate steps to deal with problems at hand. The notion of taking questions was on track—but this should have been done in advance.

His opening statements should have made clear that he was well aware of the audience's concerns, understood, and was taking further action immediately to handle the issues at hand. He needed to make a quick, direct, honest, decisive response to an obvious catastrophe. This participant felt sorry for him, and about the whole predicament for everyone involved. Totally upsetting.

Don't wander into a hostile situation meek and innocent when you know you or one of your team members made a glaring mistake.

To get a handle on what might occur in the above example, the executive as well as members of his staff and local congregation leaders could have contacted key members of the group in advance, assessed their thoughts and feelings, figured out a way to express their concerns and acknowledge the anger and resentment. Only then, in this observer's judgment, could he begin to outline what was being done to try to make things right.

Improper?

Do not assume there's some unwritten social contract that says advance contact with audience members is "improper." That's not true, and it's a lame excuse when you know better. Reach out to key individuals in advance when it's evident that there's a problem. Explain that you want to hear their point of view. If you don't have answers yet, it's OK to say you're working on it, and that you look forward to getting back to the group.

With tact, caution, and mindfulness, you'll find that people you contact in advance usually will "get" your concern and will want to help you be well prepared. If they don't, press on, try someone else.

The official mentioned above was asked during that session to apologize for the crisis at hand. He did apologize, arguably the problem was not his fault, but someone in charge had to take responsibility. He could have apologized much more effectively at the outset.

It's hard to apologize when you're caught by surprise, unprepared. Fight or flight is a natural tendency when you're trapped. Sometimes life is not fair. Sometimes people you should be able to trust lack common sense or have revenge in mind, rather than considering what's good for everyone involved, what will work best in the long run.

Take steps to prepare as much as is reasonable on short notice, so you can do the right thing. Do your best, and move on.

In truth, sometimes the one in charge has to take some punishment, be resilient, press on and work on longer-term solutions. No one in their right mind would say that being a top executive in charge is always easy. Get over it and move on as best you can.

Make Structural Adjustments

Even if it means skipping over some prepared remarks, in facing an adversarial audience, get right to the issues and challenges at hand, deal with them directly.

"In facing an adversarial audience, get right to the issues and challenges at hand and deal with them directly."

Otherwise your listeners will hear very little, get more and more impatient, and reject what you have to say.

You may never face a situation quite as extreme, and may not need to give an apology, as did the church official. But you may have to tackle an especially uncomfortable issue assertively—tactfully, directly, but not aggressively—from the start.

Unbundle

If the situation involves a bundle of hostile questions, it is best to quickly unbundle them if possible into a sequence of key topics, and provide short, direct responses to each point. Then finish with a summary, and a conclusion on as positive a note as you reasonably can.

Finally, there may be questions that *cannot* be answered on the spot. Say so, and come equipped to take questions in order to get back to people later, through some reasonable channel. Depending on the situation, this could mean to return in person, to make an online connection, or—perhaps best—to write a written response delivered to everyone in the organization. Don't over-promise, yet be as thorough as you reasonably can in following up.

Security

Of course, all of this presupposes a level of personal safety for you and for your team in such public appearances. Especially for an executive of a large corporation or a major organization, security measures from minimal to very high could be in order. High security may mean the use of private security professionals, the organization's own security team, or the use of off-duty police officers. Don't be naive about this.

In my initial public relations duties for a major telecommunications corporation and then for a major bank, sometimes our team asked professional security to be there "just in case." The dangers at the time simmered down with no harmful consequences, but things don't always go that way.

In many if not most cases, it pays to face an unfriendly but manageable audience. Such an appearance can fuel knowledge, insight, and mutual understanding, and begin to turn public opinion to your advantage, even lead to increased community support for your organization.

CHAPTER 32

Get Useful Audience Feedback

Getting valuable feedback about your speech or presentation often just doesn't get done. It's always a relief for a speaker to finish and be able to move on to whatever's next. Why not just forget about that speech and take a break for a while?

Two Good Reasons Why

First, if your approach to public speaking is too passive, only a matter of duty "when you have to," you may be missing major opportunities for your business, for your employees, for the community, and for yourself. Even in this day of social media, not much compares with the degree to which your public speaking can directly influence your market, your customers, your team, and your reputation as a leader.

Second, a significant amount of feedback—at least from the program or event chair—about the talk you just gave can be a powerful starting point for your next speech as well as help you improve your writing and delivery skills in general so that the feedback is worth your while.

Qualitative, Quantitative

My clients always appreciate getting quantitative and qualitative feedback as soon as possible. Quantitative feedback includes scaled-response questions to get "ratings," for example, scores on the speech overall, on specific points, on delivery, and perhaps also on your use of visuals. A 0–10-point scale works well, with 0 as the lowest point or "very poor," and 10 as "excellent." Technically, statistically this is a good approach. As a practical matter, this always worked well for this professional.

Such a scorecard can be quite useful, but too often the interviewee will be too polite, not at all objective, afraid to offend. Be wary of undue, overly kind positives—they won't help you improve your public speaking. At the same time, you can press the point a bit for criticism, but don't make your contact uncomfortable.

Particularly helpful and more objective could be to have an associate ask such questions for you, as well as asking a few open-ended questions, probing how people feel about you as a speaker, about your message, and about your organization. How did your listeners feel about your talk? Do they still have basic questions they'd ask? Might they actually intend to do something new because of what you had to say?

Try for Three Sources

In my experience, getting feedback by phone usually works well enough. Try to reach at least three audience representatives within a week after your speech.

Some breadth of perspective adds balance to the picture, but you likely don't need a large sample of interviewees. The judgment of a good program or event chair and two or three more individuals—perhaps people you talked with in your advance research—may be useful enough. Watch for patterns in what's said. If some points are contradictory, you always could try to reach one or two other individuals for their opinions.

Useful Follow-Up Questions

A particularly useful qualitative follow-up question is, "What one story, concept, or idea seemed to be of particular interest to you or the audience overall?" The answer can reveal what worked especially well, and can identify elements you could emphasize more in your next speech.

Another useful item is "Were any questions not answered well? Did you yourself have a question you wished could have been addressed?" (This is useful language in professional market research.)

For Your Next Speech

When you prepare for a similar talk upcoming, feedback from your most recent speech can help you get started on what to say and how to say it, sensitive points to investigate, and elements you could drop, clarify, or add.

Yet check the point of view of your new listeners and how they may tend to think about your topic, as well as words and phrases they may use to express themselves about your topic. Their views might be unique. Just a couple of phone calls in advance could suffice.

Outreach

CHAPTER 33

Community Outreach as Strategy

Have you ever noticed that leaders who make it to the top and develop strong leadership stature tend to be good at public speaking? Although this author has no wide-ranging data about this, it seems that, in business leadership succession, often the emergent top executive is an accomplished public speaker. This is one reason for any aspiring executive to pay attention to the points advocated in this book.

If you already are at the top, you still can master these skills—the sooner the better. You likely will have an opportunity to advocate a new vision, especially at times of crisis—and skillful public speaking can make all the difference in your leadership. Sometimes there's a major sea change "out there," such as the pandemic we've seen, or the quick emergence of the virtual era today.

It can be essential for a top executive to be able to reach out effectively to community audiences—as a respected leader—about what's going on, about what has changed, about new initiatives, and about what the organization is doing to catch up or get ahead of the curve.

Clearly, in dealing with the COVID pandemic and during major challenges in the economy, the general public has looked to top executives, not just elected officials, to be leaders not only in their own organization, but also in the community. For your company or not-for-profit team, your customers, investors or donors, employees and job applicants, trainees, and the media can have a stake in what's happening, and what might ensue: corrections, new possibilities, opportunities for the future.

When it comes to outreach to the general public, there's a much bigger concern today, at least in the United States. As political scientist and sociologist R.D. Putnam has observed with convincing data, "Since the 1960s America has become steadily less equal, more polarized ... fragmented ... individualistic."[1] He bases this on data from 1895 to 2015, and calls for change today to rebuild ties between the individual and the community—"fashioning an American 'we' that is sustainable because it is inclusive."[2]

To relate to Putnam's "we-ness"[3] let's consider the concept of "community ties" as investigated and reported extensively by communications scientist Stamm[4] and colleagues. This is rooted in research by Janowitz,[5] tied to initial work by sociologist Hillery[6] and his subsequent research,[7] and more recent research by this author.[8] Stamm's review has included work with L. Fortini-Campbell[9] identifying various ways an individual, a family, or a household could be tied to a community. Essentially the same could be true for a business or a not-for-profit organization; the research identifies ties to a community as "a place, a structure, or a process."

Introducing the term "link" in the context of community ties, Stamm[10] went on to ask, "Of what does a link consist?"[11] He said an individual—and presumably a company or a not-for-profit organization—could be linked to a community "spatially, cognitively, affectively, and communicatively." A spatial link could be exemplified by physical location, such as ownership of property. A cognitive link could be "community identification," whereby business owners identify themselves as a part of the community. An affective link could be one's feeling "closeness" to the community. A communication link, particularly in our context here, could be an executive speech to a public audience.

On the other hand, Stamm asked, what exists before there are links? He noted, "In the absence of community ties we have missing links, or 'gaps,'" as specified by Carter.[12] Significant for us, in the context of giving public speeches, are your opportunities to construct ties through "bridging" such gaps.[13]

"Gap Analysis" for Outreach Planning

In planning your public-speech outreach to communities, your challenge can be to identify relevant, specific gaps—such as spatial, policy, social, and information gaps that are priorities, if not also issues, for your business organization.

To do so, ask some key questions:

- Regarding spatial gaps, do public groups in your home community or in key markets even know where your business is, where your key operations are, and where to do business with your organization? Has your executive team ignored visiting key locations strategically important to your organization's future?
- Are there policy gaps between your organization and policy-making groups you should be in touch with to ward off trouble, or encourage positive outcomes? Such gaps could involve governmental policies regarding zoning and taxation,

relationships with offshore suppliers and markets, relationships with educational institutions and church organizations, and regulations dealing with health, safety, and environmental sustainability.

- What social gaps need to be addressed? Are there emergent gaps in terms of poverty, wages, ethnicity, gender, and generational interests and values?
- When it comes to "information gaps," many would come hand in hand with the above examples, but there can be a whole host of additional elements. Should your enterprise establish formal connections with new online media and user groups—community forums that online media follow, virtual communities that track your team, your products, and your services?

Business Reasons for Getting Out to Speak

Should you be seen as being in touch with the community, making an effort to communicate directly with community members? Yes, of course, particularly if you want to develop contacts, attract clients and customers, as well as new employees, and have your organization be consulted about issues affecting the business community.

Is it good for a business speaker like you to be seen as being involved in major community forums? Yes, you don't want to be thought of as aloof and uncaring. That might lead to protests, if not worse consequences such as zoning changes, new infrastructure requirements for your operations, and new taxes.

Some of the best business reasons for getting out to speak to public audiences include engaging directly with customers, making new contacts, and meeting prospects in a non-sales setting that opens the door to questions, conversations, useful feedback and ideas, and enduring connections. Other reasons for talking to public audiences can include introducing and endorsing your local operations team, responding to major public concerns, and taking a stand wisely on plans for community development.

Additional motives could include calling attention to longer-term issues of particular interest to key organizations you deal with, testing and fine-tuning your brand messaging, introducing new products and services, deepening understanding of major concerns and public issues. Furthermore, public speaking develops personal skills for leading your organization and inspiring your team to deal with new challenges and opportunities with great aplomb.

In other words, what could be crucial for you and your organization in all of this is your ability to generate confidence in you, your vision, and your leadership team among key stakeholders, including major investors, customers, and, albeit indirectly, employees and their families.

Objections to Public Speaking

A typical objection by business leaders to public speaking is that public speaking takes up too much time, and incurs unnecessary expense. Often unsaid is that, just like for most anyone, public speaking is said to be one of our greatest fears, and it can be awkward, fatiguing, and unnerving (at least at first).

Don't be swayed by the above excuses. Upon closer consideration you may realize that you and your organization can benefit substantially by reaching out to key stakeholders—and that you can handle it. You can learn to be as good a public speaker as well as anyone else regardless of your age, your current skills, and your immediate opportunities—many others have done so, and so can you—if you set your mind to it.

Outreach and Leadership

Consider a simple, down-to-earth thought that can help you develop strength when you do get out to speak. See yourself as reaching out over the lectern … to greet each person in the audience with a handshake … to take them "on a walk" with you … to see how they are doing … to share a story or two … and to make a difference in a good way as best you can.

Such a picture of reaching out to someone, can help considerably, taking the focus off of yourself, and putting it on helping someone else.

This is a tall mix of confidence, seasoned humility, and firm intention, but in my experience you can do it and it works.

Even in this day of instant digital communication and social media, skill in public speaking, especially in-person, is crucial. If you take time to develop skills for virtual and in-person public speaking, and get out and speak regularly, your efforts and your organization will be rewarded.

In the long run, your days as a leader in business will be more insightful, more effective, and much more rewarding.

CHAPTER 34

Unique "Leaderly" Opportunities

In public speaking, what should a business executive or not-for-profit leader be able to handle at least with a reasonable level of skill? The following are essentials for any CEO, board chair, president, executive director, or anyone with top leadership duties or aspirations.

Let's examine each type of speech event listed below, and consider a few basics on what it takes to be effective.

Introducing Speakers at Meetings and Formal Events

Consider one executive who sought to be the regular introducer of speakers at formal meetings of a major professional organization in his industry. He made a strategic decision to do this. His ongoing role allowed him to gain visibility for his company, and for his role as a strong leader, while not taking a lot of time to prepare full-length speeches.

His audiences came to enjoy the efficient and engaging style he learned to develop. As a presider-introducer, he interacted with other leaders in the industry, met potential clients, earned new business, and was able to spotlight members of his company team (especially his sales force) discreetly during the organization's special events.

How to Introduce a Speaker

Whether you're a veteran or an up-and-comer, you should be able to introduce a speaker in a way that draws the attention and interest of the audience, positions the speaker to do well, does not take too much time, and makes you look like a true leader. Seriously, most introductions are disorganized and take too long—and do little for the speaker, the audience, or the introducer. Make your appearance effective by sticking to these basics:

- Do not just read aloud the speaker's bio.
- Make the introduction no longer than one and a half minutes; shorter usually is better.
- Give the person's business title or position, his/her name (say the name clearly), and the topic the speaker will cover.
- Expand a bit on why the topic is relevant, and perhaps mention a point about which you know the speaker has particular expertise and the audience has definite interest.
- Quickly summarize highlights of the speaker's business credentials and background, including education.
- Near the end, repeat the speaker's name (an audience member may have just walked in and not know who the speaker is), and the topic or title of the speech.
- In a formal or semi-formal setting, add, "Please join me in welcoming _____," and lead the applause. (Redundancy in mentioning the name is good.)

Take another look at the sample introductory script in Chapter 25.

The "Impromptu" Speech

Often a business or community leader is called on to give a briefing, not just a greeting, or at least to just "say a few words," often in a context or situation where a specific message and a call to action are paramount. Seize the opportunity:

- Capture if you can the interest or needs of the audience by going quickly into a fundamental thought that will resonate with the audience and achieve the effect you intend.
- To make this work, be sure to use basic structure: after a brief opening comment or at least a thank you, state your theme in one sentence, delivering your message with three supporting components to back it up, and add a conclusion related to your theme, perhaps calling for continued or new action by your audience.
- The overall length might be three to five minutes, no more than seven minutes. Don't ramble; stick to your key points.
- Such a talk can be a simple message that brings the matter at hand into sharp focus, pulls everyone together, and leads into something positive.

In advance, if you feel you may be asked to give a short talk like this, give it some thought, think about main points carefully, and—if you have a couple of minutes—giving at least part of it a practice run-through.

There can be considerable "magic" in the five- to seven-minute talk. Although it's relatively brief, you can deliver a message that is substantial.

A Conference Speech

Good executives—especially individuals with unusual expertise or who have earned a high level of respect—often are called on to give a conference speech, if not a keynote address (usually that's reserved for a senior executive). We've mentioned this in previous chapters, but let's reconsider a few highlights:

- Your most valuable contacts at the outset and throughout the process are the conference chair, and the conference committee if there is one. Talk to them in advance. Ask them for names of good representatives of the audience and chat with a couple of those individuals in advance also, if possible. Get their point of view about the conference and about your topic, including questions they might ask you if they could.
- Often a conference chair will ask a guest speaker for a longer speech than need be. Leave time for questions. Recognize that introductions and agenda-setting for the day will take up some of the time that's supposedly yours. A one-hour speech on the agenda usually means 50 minutes, allowing for a short break in between sessions. Taking away announcements and a too-long introduction leaves 45–47 minutes. If it's at all possible (if the room works for this, if the audience is not too large), leave 10 minutes for Q&A. That leaves approximately 35–37 minutes of solid material. That's not so daunting.
- If you tighten your speech and have significant things to say, along with a couple of entertaining stories where the humor is self-deprecating and politically correct, the audience will like you.
- Don't try to be a comedian (wastes people's time) unless you are one.
- At the close, after the Q&A, wrap up with a crisp summary restating the conclusion of the speech. Punchy and short works best. Stop and step back; don't thank the audience, let them thank you with applause, as they would want to do if you've done the work.

Don't Forget

Consider these further points to make your efforts worthwhile:

- With at least some humility, at the outset focus on particular interests of the audience; maybe include a point or two that will leave them wondering how you knew! Respect their time, and go for elements that can capture their interest and imagination, possibly take a stand, and definitely make a difference.

- Even with practice your speech likely will run a little longer than you expect.
- Don't just give a digital slide presentation, do not use old slides or video that may be slightly off the mark. Today's audiences expect the best. Otherwise, you'll lose the audience. Talk to them.
- Talk to them as if you were on a walk with them one-on-one.
- For most any speech, remember that the audience almost always wants you to be comfortable and succeed—so they can feel good about being there. Thus, they are on your side. Go down the road together.

CHAPTER 35

What Program Chairs Look For

Consider the views of two program chairs charged with lining up CEO speakers at regional business forums.[1] The first interviewee ("Chair 1") is a former newspaper and magazine editor, and public relations consultant, who has worked with service club program committees, and has made a point of being attuned to major business leaders in the public eye. The second interviewee ("Chair 2") is a management consultant who for years secured business and political leaders to talk to an ongoing forum attended by CEOs of companies with 20–150 employees. The format for these two was in-person speaking, but the lessons still apply to online formats.

Traits of Good Speakers

CHAIR 1: "Stature, or, if not, then a particular expertise, and the ability to talk about the industry rather than just the company, and how the industry impacts other businesses."
CHAIR 2: "They have valuable application ideas, and can give people ideas on how to apply what they are discussing. So, good stories to tell, credibility, take-backs, ideas they can demonstrate."

Credentials They Look For

CHAIR 1: "Who has had them speak, how they come across, how articulate they are, and their ability to connect the dots."
CHAIR 2: "Credibility, not necessarily front page [stature], but proven results."

Weaknesses

CHAIR 1: "A presentation [slides] so intricate you can't see them. Too many anecdotes. Trying to give a speech that the speaker had not read ahead of time."

CHAIR 2: "Oftentimes, a lack of preparation. They have sort of a 'speech' but don't give a lot of thought to the audience, don't know their audience. Overall, though, I can't think of a really poor speaker [at our forum]—I try to coach people about the event [ahead of time], what we're looking for."

Signs of a Good Speech

CHAIR 1: "Talking about their industry, not their company. Ability to rattle some cages—a CEO who is capable and comfortable."

CHAIR 2: "Someone who tends to give a 'shout out,' calling out to people in the audience by name if the speaker knows them. Someone who connects with people in the audience, as in 'I've been there and I know you, I understand you, I'm one of you.' Also, having some kind of application to business—insight, ideas such that [the listener concludes] 'I should think about that, I should do that.' Action points people can get excited about and consider doing."

Preparation That Counts

CHAIR 1: "Enough to be able to field questions, to be an 'open book,' to be able to entertain questions at the end of the talk. Also, to be able to say, 'I don't know and I'm not going to wing it.' These are powerful words."

CHAIR 2: "Knowing the audience, knowing what issues are most important to them."

About Delivery

CHAIR 1: "A certain humility is a good thing. It humanizes the speaker to be able to say, for example, that sometimes these numbers may not mean much to you, but bean counters like us pay attention to them."

CHAIR 2: "Speakers need to rehearse a lot, so they are not stumbling over their own written remarks. It's better to be the person you are than who you're not—if you are a dark suit, a formal person, then be that way.

"Sometimes visuals are not as effective as having no visuals. In slides, trend lines on slides are very helpful, as long as the trendlines are big enough to be clear. Videos are kind of boring, and there are fewer than there used to be. I find them distracting. Internet-link visuals, social media can be relevant, but I find that a flier or handout with such links is more helpful. As far as a handout, make it one page, but it depends. For example, if the CEO of a CPA firm has a good summary of new laws and regulations, a booklet prepared for clients, then that can work.

"There's a trend toward using fewer slides. There's use of videos but I don't care for it, they're a technical distraction. Videos sort of stop everything. They tend to be promotional, something PR put together for the CEO, and so they tend to weaken the presentation. Often people bring PowerPoints, set up with a thumb drive, and then get caught up in their slides instead of first connecting with at least some of the people in the room before starting the talk."

Other Suggestions

CHAIR 1: "It depends on what the speaker is trying to accomplish—to communicate something in particular, to become more well known, more prominent? It's a little less self-aggrandizing if, to begin with, someone approaches the group on behalf of the speaker.

"A group like ours should know in advance why the CEO would be interesting and appropriate for the group. You want to be as pertinent and as appropriate as possible. One prominent speaker asked me in the beginning what I thought would be a good topic.

"Be authentic....

"After you've written the speech, read it out loud. The written word often doesn't provide shorter sentences and clear language. Read it aloud, and edit as you read.

"It's good for the CEO to ask the program chair after the fact for feedback."

CHAIR 2: "To find CEOs or other leadership speakers, I still look to the headlines, but am more interested in someone I've heard about and has a story to tell."

In Conclusion

These real-world comments, echoing many of the points we've covered so far, can help anyone intending to reach out and speak convincingly to major public audiences.

CHAPTER 36

A "Rollout"

Let's consider a scenario exemplifying how to launch an executive's visibility and public speaking outreach for the longer term. This is meant to exemplify a typical situation facing a new corporate CEO, or the head of a not-for-profit or civic organization, or any major enterprise.

A New Executive

Many if not most companies at one point need to introduce a new senior executive who may be an heir apparent to the current CEO. Let's assume the new senior executive is neither well-known to the public, nor to a good number of the company's employees. The following story is based on an actual experience, but the names and circumstances are altered to protect individual and company privacy.

The company was a regional service provider with markets and customers at the community, local, regional, and national levels. The current CEO was due to retire in three to five years, and the newly appointed president and heir-apparent had an impressive sales background. Yet there was a problem. Although a leader in sales, he had little experience with public speaking to community audiences and was not comfortable with it.

He needed and wanted to develop his public speech abilities, and was open to working with speech professionals. As the corporate speechwriter at the time, this author had assisted a variety of other senior executives in the company for several years, and relished the opportunity to help the new president become a "superstar."

Step One: Training

Our first step was to line up training involving a speech-delivery coach as well as the speechwriter to work on basic public-speaking delivery. This avoided the trap set unwittingly by many public relations practitioners of giving a new executive "media training" only, but not actual training in public speaking. This seems to be a common mistake because many public relations practitioners assume that being able to handle tough media questions is all that's needed for public appearances, public speaking included. Such an executive may indeed need media training, but that's different.

Underlying all this is that interaction with a reporter indeed can be adversarial; public speaking is usually about establishing a positive relationship with an audience, as we've indicated repeatedly—a huge difference that needs to be taken into account.

As should be obvious to you by now, delivering speeches is a unique skillset, and content and delivery should fit together hand in glove to be successful.

Working with a speech-delivery trainer—as well as with a speechwriter—should include reviewing what speech training you've had, correcting any wrong impressions of what to do, and then focusing on fundamentals for key situations. This also should include an opportunity to see yourself speaking, and making improvements, on camera, with digital video that you can take with you and review later. Trial and error in such formal instruction can be humbling, but will lead to enhancing your speech performance considerably.

Even though in many cases your speechwriter could also serve as the trainer, using a delivery coach and a speechwriter works best for initial basic training. In my experience, a delivery coach with video-production experience is ideal.

Being included in the delivery training helps the writer get to know more about the client's background, interests, favorite expressions, and often useful stories as well. This setup lets the speechwriter raise questions about executive annoyances, concerns, and preferences—and appreciate the executive's strengths. It's also good for teamwork to hear about situations the client has worried about in the past, to make sure the person gets a chance to work on such concerns during the training session.

This arrangement also can help the executive get to know what the writer has to offer, put them on the same wavelength, begin brainstorming new ideas, check any unclear recommendations the trainer makes, and get going on working together on an upcoming speech opportunity.

A significant challenge in all this is getting the person to be trained to an isolated location for at least half a day to work on speech skills. Half a day is enough time to cover three key typical situations: (1) speaking to a small group, perhaps an employee group, (2) to a larger, public speech forum such as a breakfast or luncheon, and (3) then at a more formal occasion, such as a dinner or conference speech.

Typically, there never is a second chance to work together quite like this, so the trainer and this author strived to make it all happen well and efficiently in one session. That three-part sequence made it possible to establish positive experiences and identify specific skills and content that could work well in each situation, as well as points that could apply anytime.

For an early-morning training session, which usually is best, it helps if the session starts early enough to allow finishing perhaps by 11:30 a.m., so that the executive can check in with an assistant and return key phone calls before lunch. Late afternoon also could work for training, but generally at that time of day there end up being too many delays and interruptions.

Step Two: Developing a First Basic Speech

During the training session the good speechwriter may begin to think through elements of a basic speech that could work for the executive especially well, including a story or two that could be used later.

During the training session for the executive in this "rollout" example, it quickly became apparent that one of his goals was to encourage all employees to pay more attention to customers, helping employees reach out more engagingly to achieve a higher level of service excellence for the company overall.

Initial research by this writer with three or four carefully chosen representatives of the first audience the speaker was scheduled to address had found that many in that group faced challenges in sales and service similar to what the new president had dealt with. With a little prompting in the training session, we got him talking about the "taxicab shoe malfunction" reported in a previous chapter. We immediately saw this as a natural tie-in with the service theme.

Out of all this came a basic speech that addressed basic business challenges with the president's new approach, let him use his self-deprecating personal story that was fun in the telling, and increased his public-speaking confidence. He enjoyed acting out the cab scene—and it opened the door for this new president to introduce some of his many innovative ideas for improving customer service. The resulting speech combined all these factors into a talk that was sincere, fun to listen to, and introduced new practices the company wanted to publicize. Perfect!

Step Three: Once-a-Month Appearances

Since the speechwriter may already have in mind potential audiences for such a speaker, it can be possible to quickly lay out a path leading from smaller, "easier" audiences gradually into larger, more prestigious forums. Depending on the skills and strengths of the speaker, and the speech writer/coordinator, identifying appropriate forums may take careful research. In our case framing a worthwhile path worked out especially well. Along the road we found that setting up a good forum for this new president once a month on average fostered a good learning curve for making progress in public speaking, and covered several key audiences.

A Delicate Balance

In all of this, the speechwriter may need to deal with big aspirations, bigger time constraints, and an even larger degree of mistrust by other executives either envious or not understanding what is going on. It may not be clear to the management team at the outset how such training and early work with speech pros can lead to many benefits for the company overall.

On more than one occasion, this speechwriter encountered objections from other senior executives on an executive speaker's team who were critical about having a speechwriter in the picture. It's also common to see senior public relations managers have a hard time letting go of hands-on contact with senior executives so that a speechwriter can do his or her best for the speaker. It's all challenging—but persistence pays off.

In the bigger picture of all this, a good speechwriter's services can and should include developing a potential schedule of worthwhile speeches for the executive(s), lining up invitations, conducting thoughtful initial research, establishing a reliable structure for each speech, developing the script, working through the logistics with diligence, identifying opportunities for media coverage if appropriate and working with media relations staff about that, rehearsing the speaker, and making further use of each speech script by sharing it at least internally as appropriate.

Such teamwork on a rollout can lead to benefits not only for management and the company team, but also for a wide variety of stakeholders, especially customers (hey, it's business) and other members of the community.

Did It Work?

With such focus and dedicated effort, this rollout worked very well. This author fortunately has seen such efforts succeed with a variety of executives, younger and older, female and male, in terms of equity, persons with a variety of career backgrounds, in several companies, including small businesses and not-for-profit organizations.

The new president in our example experienced growing demand as a public speaker, and came to relish every public-speaking opportunity. He offered his service teams a strength of advocacy that served them well, especially when he took over as CEO.

Special Events

CHAPTER 37

Interviews: What Conference Organizers Look For

Let's consider the point of view of organizers of business and industry conferences. What do they look for in an executive speaker? Let's consider two veteran conference organizers—interviewed here in some detail.[1]

Organizer #1 had a depth of experience organizing conferences for mortgage lenders, working directly with a variety of CEO speakers, and is an accomplished public speaker himself. Organizer #2 served as a director for an association of CPAs.

Traits of a Top Executive Speaker

ORGANIZER 1: "Top speakers can talk not only about their company but as an industry expert on a specific subject within the industry, and can set the stage to establish credibility right away, in terms of background and experience, so the audience believes what the speaker has to say."

ORGANIZER 2: "'Notoriety'—somebody that will get them in the door.... If the listeners can see that speakers will know what they are talking about, that they're experts in their field. If a CEO wants to do this as a marketing opportunity, I tell them that it has to be only in the first two minutes or in the last two minutes. A conference speech has to be an education session."

Hallmarks of a Good Keynote

ORGANIZER 1: "It really comes down to the conference committee, what direction they want a keynoter to take, being aware of the direction the committee is going.... A conference has a theme. If a speaker is an industry expert, the speaker shouldn't talk about 'our company' and 'why we are great.' Balance that out with industry and company examples—'Here's what we did'—but not making that the focus of the remarks. Also, knowing who the audience is, knowing their specific role [in the conference]."

155

ORGANIZER 2: "For a keynote, something that pulls at the heartstrings, to
have listeners react and think at a level that they don't normally think. In
connecting with the audience there has to be a part of you in the speech,
you have to have a passion. Talk about your struggles, too, something
that can connect the audience to you at that 'everyday' level."

Speaker Strengths

ORGANIZER 1: "For any speaker, particularly a CEO, knowing the subject
better than the audience does, being as prepared as the person can be.
Also, good eye contact, completing sentences, being concise, not being
a windbag. Knowing what they will cover, and covering the material
within the time frame. And being able to control the audience—perhaps
answering questions as they go, but if there are too many taking too long,
then saying 'We'll come back to that in the Q&A.'"

ORGANIZER 2: "Good 'application' ideas that people can use. Good stories
to tell. Personality! They've got to 'run' the audience with the confidence,
to be able to 'tell them what you want to tell them' so they understand.
Presence on stage."

Weaknesses

ORGANIZER 1: "If they avoid most of the questions, if they are not specific.
Yet it's fine to say you'll check with your experts and then get back to the
listeners.... Is the speaker a manager or leader? A leader inspires others, a
manager knows the details. We expect the leader to know where to go to
find that answer.

"If they 'read' the speech with no eye contact, people lose confidence.
Practice before getting to the live crowd. Don't talk too fast, don't use
industry jargon."

ORGANIZER 2: "If you're going to use a slide, make it simple. If you refer to a
tax code or such, make it simple—people are not there to read [details on]
a slide. In slides use a bigger font. Actually, rather than depending on a
slide, you're better off just explaining what you are trying to tell them.

"While using slides, engage the audience rather than looking down at
a copy, or reading each slide [to the audience] the whole time."

Elements of a Good Speech

ORGANIZER 1: "If you want to open with humor or anecdotes, stay away
from jokes focusing on a particular group.

"If you're going to talk about a particular experience, then do it—tell
them what you're going to tell them, do it, then conclude by explaining
why it's significant, maybe reviewing a couple of key points.

"If you're a keynoter, be open to at least a brief Q&A period at the end, or have someone from the committee get three or four questions from the audience for you.

"Start off with something strong—serious or motivational—and finish with something strong. Keep them [the audience] energized. Have a destination where you want people to go, what they should do, and why it's good to do so.

"In delivery, step to the side of the lectern from time to time. That opens yourself up to the audience. Talk to this section [of the audience], and then that section, a little bit. This engages people, as in 'I'm having a conversation with you.'"

ORGANIZER 2: "In the first couple of sentences what they say to connect with the audience is crucial."

What Preparation Helps

ORGANIZER 1: "It's probably good to develop an outline and send it off to the committee, asking if it's what they had in mind for their audience. Know your subject as well as you can, better than anyone else in the room. Rehearse your talk in front of a mirror, and with colleagues.

"At our company, in practices, we get a big Mason #10 jar, and a colleague will drop a penny in the jar—you can really hear it—every time the speaker says an 'um' or 'ah' or 'you know' or some such verbal pause. You become amazed at how often you do these things. If you learn to just pause, people think it's a 'dramatic pause' that you intended. Learn not to roll a pencil or pen in your hand, or have your hands in your pockets—very distracting."

ORGANIZER 2: "Know your audience. For example, CPAs are not 'accountants,' they are CPAs.

"One speaker learned the committee members' names, and in speaking would call out to each of them, asking each a question, but having told them in advance what question he would ask."

Noticeable Trends

ORGANIZER 1: "Using fewer and simpler digital slides. One national-level speaker used all pictures instead of word slides. Cartoons, like *New Yorker* cartoons, are great.

"People try to get away from using slides. Video is great—if it's brief, 45 seconds.

"By the way, in using slides, never turn your back to the audience to read bullet points—have your laptop in front of you to see what the audience is seeing."

ORGANIZER 2: "If there's someone you want people to meet, use online conferencing to introduce the person to the audience and have [just] a brief conversation."

Further Suggestions

ORGANIZER 1: "Three points: A. Know the audience, who it is that you can tailor your remarks to. B. Know your subject matter. C. Practice the delivery."

ORGANIZER 2: "If your stopping time is 10 o'clock, stop at 10 or people will lose your message—this is huge.

"Keep the politics out. Don't tell stories related to sex, gender, race, something your wife or husband did—that's sexist. Your message gets lost."

In Addition

ORGANIZER 1: "You could talk about something that just didn't work. Being willing to 'hang yourself out there' gets respect. Explain what didn't work and why.... Be a 'statesman' rather than a 'politician.' A statesman advocates what's best for people and doesn't need everyone to agree."

ORGANIZER 2: "In advance, in trying to get invited to speak, be able to send a good five-minute video clip [demonstrating your ability as a speaker] that's clear and concise. This and maybe a couple of phone calls is about all I need to judge if a speaker would be good for our conference."

CHAPTER 38

Serving on a Panel

What does it take to do well in a panel discussion? Let's consider the perspective of the executive director of a major civic organization that has covered a wide range of public policy, economic, environmental, and business issues—often by way of panel discussions. The context here is in-person, but most points would apply to an online forum as well.[1]

Focus

"Program committees for our organization," this executive director said, "look for executive-level input on 'community engagement' about major issues. The point is to provide thought-leader views, insights, and direction to the organization's members and guests."

A Good Panel...

Typically, there are "three or fewer" individuals on a panel, she noted. "If there are more, the discussion tends to be 'sound bites' rather than substantive remarks and thoughtful, reflective comments," she said.

As for types of panelists, "Diversity is key—it's all about the wisdom of the community emerging from different perspectives. Diversity in terms of gender, age, political perspectives, professional associations, government, the academic world, different points of view."

The Moderator

"The moderator is the key to everything," she said, "the perspective of the moderator and the intelligence of the moderator. So we look for familiarity with the topic, depth, the ability to take a conversation and follow it if someone says something provocative. A good moderator can lead the audience and support the conversation."

The Goal of Having a Panel

For an effective program, the goal is "creating a good chemistry, and letting it happen. It's so important that the session be 'spontaneous,' and that there be some 'levity.' To begin, we usually get right into questions, looking for different approaches, spontaneity of the moment. Rarely do we begin with formal opening remarks by the panelists," she said.

Desirable Panelists

"Good panelists know who the audience is, what's relevant, care about the audience, spark off a question that comes up. Someone who has a great subject knowledge but also with experience knowledge, having walked that road before," the executive director said.

Key traits: "Frankness, honesty, a behind-the-scenes perspective, timeliness. Someone who listens to the other panelists. What stands out is 'the quality of reflection'—how that person incorporates that in the topic at hand, connects to other issues, other trends," she said. "This is rare!"

Preparation

To prepare well, she said, "it's thinking through who this audience is, what they are expecting." As for preparing about the topic itself, "your preparation is your whole life experience." Also important are "willing-ness to be controversial," and "learning more about the sponsoring orga-nization to get as much context as possible.... It's good to know who the other panelists are."

Great Panelists

- "The best is someone able to move beyond his or her expertise and make connections, even discuss a point he or she changed their mind about and why."
- "The more people feel conversant or comfortable with their own expertise the more they are able to connect with others."

- "Someone who really listens to questions, talks about what's down the road, takes it to the next level."

Some Observations

Note that this individual's recommendations begin and end with focusing on the audience, and on "listening." Also, a fundamental Questioning Tactic at play here is "problem solving," which is quite common in a panel discussion.

Our next chapter summarizes another interview with a pro about serving as a panelist.

CHAPTER 39

Another Perspective on Panels

Since serving as a speaker or moderator on a panel can be so uncharted and unpredictable, let's look at a somewhat different situation, and the views of a thought-leader and conference coordinator in financial services.[1] In the previous chapter our focus was on someone hosting forums on a regular basis. This interviewee explains that running a special-purpose conference can be a somewhat different matter.

A Panelist, Not Just a Speaker

"A panel can deliver strength through a diversity of opinions," the coordinator said. "The point is to get as much information and opinion out to the audience as possible, not just an advertisement for a speaker's company.... What works especially well is a panel that entails engaging conversation. This can happen especially if there is a really strong moderator who knows the subject, ideally someone who can move the conversation, not letting one individual dominate."

The Chemistry

A combination of panelists works best if they all "talk the same talk, are related but different, speak the same language, are peer-level, and have the same background. And the moderator should be one of their peers. I've seen some panels where you wonder what the connection is between these people."

A Good Panelist

"Is it someone who knows the subject matter? And you have to talk with them beforehand to judge if the person would be forthcoming or not.

It doesn't work to have someone who falls back on 'I can't tell you that because it's a trade secret.' The point is to educate, inform the audience, so the panelist has to be knowledgeable—and willing to be forthcoming," the conference coordinator said.

This coordinator has learned to be selective in choosing panelists, and sometimes says no. "If in the pre-interview a potential panelist doesn't want to 'tell,' doesn't want to answer questions straightforwardly," he said, "then that person will not be cooperative, and will take the luster off.

"Indeed, if you are making arrangements for yourself, your CEO, or your client, take a close look at the other panelists before you commit. It could be easy to get into an unfavorable situation," the coordinator said.

A "Peer" Moderator Is Best

Again, the moderator can make a very positive difference, especially when he or she is a peer among peers. The coordinator said, "The moderator can ask the same question of one or two panelists, but not each one. If the panelists and the moderator are of the same level, the others may jump in with their own observations, like in a conversation. That adds credibility and interest for everyone.

"'Peer-level' in this case can mean senior vice presidents, or even CEOs. Yet a CEO likely would be kept for an appearance as a keynote or featured speaker."

Salting the Audience

To promote audience participation, this organizer finds it helps to set up a couple of questions ahead of time among audience members—sometimes referred to as "salting the audience"—"to get the ball rolling," he said. Yet he keeps this to a minimum so the conversation becomes genuine and captivating. The goal, he explained, is "a lively and open conversation with plenty of energy, and a quick exchange of views."

An "Eyes Wide Open" Opportunity

As a long-time corporate public relations manager observed upon reviewing the above, "A person needs to go into a panel with eyes wide open." There are downsides that may be bigger than the upsides.

Yet visibility as a panelist can open up new opportunities, either to speak, or to develop new business. After someone not well-known in a major civic organization did an excellent job as a conference participant, it was great to see that she later was asked to be the organization's executive director!

CHAPTER 40

The Commencement Address

If giving a commencement address is on your horizon, consider the following thoughts. We've referred to this and related ideas somewhat already in previous chapters, but let's give it full attention here, from start to finish. Similar to other speech preparations, the "kickoff" is to interview college authorities and staff to get a take on their advice, needs and wishes, then perhaps to interview a few students recommended by those officials.

Best of Times, Yet Difficult

Whether to a large audience or a small group, a commencement address in many ways can be the best of times for a business leader. If selected, you're chosen based on your accomplishments, your reputation, and the faith of the school administration in what you have to offer to the students, families, and guests. So you have a leg up, for starters.

Yet the occasion isn't really much about you. For many listeners the speaker and the speech at best are only things to be tolerated. If your address is online, there can be even more of a challenge; people too easily can tune out. In any case, it's likely that at least a few listeners will remember your words of wisdom.

This author has attended four commencements as a student, and four as a parent. One commencement ceremony, for a family member, was outdoors, in the rain. Despite the dedicated effort on the speaker's part, a celebrated policy-maker and leader at the national level, it's hard to remember today even who the speaker was, much less what was said.

For a speechwriter, it's different when clients are involved; their speeches are well stamped in the writer's mind long term (what this author remembers especially are the stories they told).

Should You Agree to Do It?

Despite those negatives, a commencement address is something special. The opportunity is unmatched as an occasion for you to "give back" to your listeners. You'll be introduced with honor, and inevitably it's a happy occasion for everyone.

They need a speaker. If you're asked, make the best of it! If you do, you'll be glad you did, and you'll also have an excellent reference for further public talks.

An Even More Positive Note

Among the positives about giving a commencement address, some points are crucial. First, if you get it right you can amplify the moment as a day for the students, and help them get through it. You're their advocate. On the graduates' behalf you also can recognize and thank those who helped make the occasion possible, including paying tuition: parents, spouses, sponsors, friends. As a leader in the community, you can foster positive hopes, healthy pride, mutual understanding, good intentions, and best wishes.

"Look at you!"

For one client, speaking at a winter-quarter graduation, this speechwriter was worried about the more subdued timing (as compared with a spring main event) as well as about students using smart phones for taking "selfies" and texting during the speech, and others in the audience also multitasking, as well as too many listeners just wriggling and waiting to get through the day.

This is the CEO in an earlier chapter known among his associates for his "emotional intelligence." When we discussed the event, it was clear that he wanted to direct his attention right away to the students at the outset of his talk, which he did: "Wow! Look at you! What an exciting day. Thank you for inviting me." This note of engagement worked well for him and for his audience, and he was off to a good start.

And then, on script, he briefly touched on job markets, which were not so good at the time. "You see," he said, "everyone graduating today is smarter, works faster, and is better equipped to compete in the global job market than I was when I was sitting in your chair. You can text, search, post quickly, and use technology to improve your productivity and the productivity of the organization that is lucky enough to hire you."

Affirming the graduates' unique technical strengths early on like this struck an upbeat note that the graduates could take away as a positive.

Parents and Family

Perhaps more likely to retain the thoughts and feelings of such a day are the parents, spouses, and friends. So acknowledge them early on. For example, one CEO said spontaneously to her audience, "With your education, as my dear parents drilled into me, anything is possible. Let me suggest that graduation is a day to honor and remember our teachers, our parents, our family."

She went on, "As I reflect back, in my life I have encountered many interesting people, including mentors who have helped me. But years ago, if you told me that my most important mentor would be my grandfather, I would not have believed you." Everyone listened intently as she told the story related in a previous chapter about her grandfather.

At a graduation ceremony, picking up on endearing family ties can work especially well. Perhaps it also can be an occasion to talk about how a particular teacher or mentor changed your life.

Part of the implied assignment for the speaker is to inspire, and to take the audience to a higher level in general at least for the day. The speech may be recorded, and even could end up on the internet. So make your mark—it might endure longer than you think.

A Thought for One's Future

Your personal experiences may especially be appreciated at a small, more intimate gathering, such as a departmental ceremony at a major university before the big annual graduation. In such a setting a speaker can relate an unusual experience pertinent to particular opportunities the audience members may deal with soon. The following was a key focus by a bank executive speaking at a special, department-level commencement gathering, to graduates in economics:

> After I graduated I went to Navy Officer Candidate School—this was in the Vietnam era. My first assignment was to join an amphibious ship in Vietnam as an "engineering" officer. I managed a crew of 45 in the electrical division. How the Navy made the connection between economics, engineering, and electricity I'm still not quite sure. For me, this was an opportunity at a very young age to take a leadership position, to learn to do things through others, to depend on a team and help them depend on one another. Excellent management experience, right out of college.

A Matter of Character

He went on to add a note of inspiration from a fitting angle: "I believe 'bigheartedness' is most empowering," he said. "In light of your great heart, I ask you today to keep in mind your alma mater as you advance in your careers. As alums, consider fostering continued excellence here at this university. Let's continue to invite others into the university community, and help them succeed."

For sure, the faculty and staff loved that message.

Overall, the most inspiring speakers tend to be those who are thankful and support the long-term success not only of the graduates, but also the families and the organizations that have helped so many and could continue to do so in the future.

With Caution

As a side note, in speaking to a commencement audience be careful about what you say regarding matters that could be divisive, and be careful in using slang. A careless word or comment could come back to haunt you. Also, be cautious in your use of humor, because too often what's humorous to you is not seen that way by someone else.

Chapter 41

More Ceremonials

In addition to the commencement address, let's deal with some other ceremonial speeches.

The term can apply to a wide range of events: welcoming remarks, introductions of speakers, dedications, ribbon cuttings and unveilings, award acceptances, staff or team appreciation talks, testimonials, retirement ceremonies, even being asked during the holidays to "just say a few words." For these occasions, strive to speak conversationally, like talking to a group of good friends—but do not downplay the importance of the event.

A Mistake

In a corporate retirement ceremony, the CEO threw a company anniversary pin to a recipient, apparently trying to be informal and humorous. Big mistake. Disrespectful, wrong in every way. Fleeting moments can become permanent remembrances. Rise to the occasion, care about the people involved, make the occasion special, be kind, and be thankful you can make a positive difference in someone's life.

A Eulogy

At some point you may be asked to deliver a eulogy. Consider a recent church memorial service as an example. A senior bank executive this author knew quite well was asked to give the eulogy for a close relative of his, and agreed to give brief remarks. For this he talked about the deceased "in three chapters." Chapter one dealt with one set of memories, chapter two another, and chapter three focused on a final and especially compelling element.

As grief hung heavy in the air, it was apparent to me that his forthright, threefold chapter structure helped this speaker keep going despite a considerable mix of emotions for him personally. The simple framework gave him confidence, kept him on track, and aptly supported his sincere and loving thoughts. The talk was quite moving. A similar approach may work well for you.

In a eulogy for a close friend years ago, this author found it helpful to include a few stories about the deceased as identified in advance through conversations with close relatives. The stories said more than any adjectives, comparatives, or superlatives could ever muster.

Developmental Experience, Efficient Strategy

Here's another thought in the realm of ceremonials: be the one to introduce speakers. This can give you many new contacts, excellent visibility, and speech-delivery experience.

For developing your own skills, for broadening your management abilities, and for getting a deeper appreciation for community outreach, look into serving as the program chair of an industry association, conference, or service club! You'll get more comfortable in appearing before public audiences, and see a variety of speech styles and techniques you can turn to when you need to get out in the community and give full-blown speeches.

In choosing such a path, you do need to consider the time you'll have to invest and when you'd do so. You might consider joining—or even starting (worked for this author)—a morning group that would take less of your workday.

Further Considerations

CHAPTER 42

Again, Why Give Speeches to Public Audiences?

Truly it takes a lot of time and effort for a dedicated leader to get out and speak effectively to public audiences. Is it worth it? Let's step back and review the benefits of doing so from the point of view of a variety of business and community leaders, and in the eyes of professionals in marketing and public relations.

Division and Opportunity

As communities grow and change, as politics veer from leeway for businesses to new social programs and then back to special tax breaks for high-income earners, and then return to adding new regulatory requirements, get ready. If you haven't up to this point, you likely will need to deal with equity, racism, and homelessness, as well as climate change, reducing pollution, new energy resources, and misinformation about all of these. Be responsive, speak up for what you believe, and do what you can to bring people together to create new opportunities for your team, for your industry, and for the community.

Seize good opportunities to explain how your industry and your organization are operating in the public interest. Perhaps even at some risk and despite some discomfort—be proactive while taking care of customers, providing needed community resources, creating jobs, paying taxes, and fostering innovation. In the long run you'll be glad you did.

It's Good Business

As one new CEO client once objected, "Why should I—do you think I'm some sort of a missionary?" Together we found the answer was simply that it is good business for a widely recognized company to engage with public audiences to provide a fresh and candid view of what's happening in one's industry, to explain leadership's vision and new developments, and to be open to respond to public concerns and new opportunities.

His initial objection was somewhat tongue-in-cheek, of course, at least this author felt that was the case. His industry had struggled mightily with issues of environmental protests, new regulation, conservation, and challenges to resource management and manufacturing practices.

Yet the proof of the value of public speaking in that case was his experience in getting out in the public eye with words chosen carefully, presenting a business point of view calmly and clearly, responding to objections, and speaking in terms the audience could relate to. He found that his wisdom and engaging manner (a CEO for many good reasons) opened doors to new customers, employees, and the overall growth of the company and its industry, and a stronger reputation overall.

Giving Back

A highly regarded regional president of an international banking and financial services company made a point to address a wide variety of public audiences, especially at the community level. With her kind determination she made community involvement—"giving back to the community"—a hallmark of the company's brand and corporate culture, at least in her domain. She is known as a pacesetter for her peers at the national level and was for her team locally, is a highly-regarded board director, and has delivered visible, enduring successes in her work for the various enterprises she has served.

Investors, Reputation

One sunny day at a crosswalk in the heart of downtown Seattle, the Chairman and CEO of a regional corporation, a key client, stopped to tell me as his public speech coordinator, researcher, and writer that my job was "more important than anyone else realizes." He said his public speaking especially helped him keep in touch with the community and local investors, and hold up the value of the stock as well as the overall reputation of the company.

What's memorable was how clearly he saw the importance of the outreach we strove for together. Sometimes it's hard to get top executives to develop such vision and appreciate such outreach. My hope is that by now you get a good sense of what this is all about and how this can work for you.

Which Community, Which Executive?

Yet a difficult question still is "Speak to 'which elements' of the community?" "Should it be special interest groups or the community in general, should the level be local, statewide, regional, national or even international?" For more and more company CEOs, and not-for-profit presidents, civic officials, and business leaders in general, the answer simply is "Yes"—on a carefully planned basis. Even a world-class, international company needs to pay attention to its local city or neighborhood community—the company's own backyard. And a small enterprise today may be able to reach new markets even internationally.

Usually it's the CEO that people want to hear from. Yet one prominent, regional company very much in the public eye—to help give the CEO a break for other duties—compromised somewhat by having a C-Suite executive serve as the company's "outside" voice.

This individual ("executive vice president" was the title) was already involved in a wide variety of community and regional groups at various levels, and had been throughout his career. So when asked, he was a natural to step up as a key spokesperson for the entire executive team and the company in general. It was apparent that he kept in good rapport with the CEO, was highly respected, widely sought after, and especially successful in community engagement on behalf of everyone in the company at that time.

Reach Out

Reconsidering what was pointed out in the preface of this book, seeing that today we are in a world and a nation so divided, with too many citizens so disconnected from one another, public understanding of companies and organizations so disordered, and international crises afoot left and right, it's essential that you and your peers in business, not-for-profits, and civic leadership reach out to the general public. This helps keep the doors of interaction open, maintain public support of mutually beneficial exchange of goods and services, fosters cooperation and mutual respect, supports the lively economy so many today have grown up with, and can spread such benefits to those who are left behind, as well as future generations to come.

Aloof Doesn't Work Long Term

As communities grow and change, as politics veer back and forth from more leeway for businesses to new social programs, and as we deal with such issues as climate change, racism, and homelessness, as well as challenges to democracy and sensible economics, it's essential for leaders like you to join the dialogue—and keep the conversation constructive.

Be responsive, speak up for what you believe, do what you can to bring people together and to create new opportunities for your team, for your industry, and for the community. We need businesses' commitment to taking care of customers, fostering innovation, creating jobs, paying fair taxes, and providing needed resources—doing the right thing.

You're the One

For company or organization outreach to such audiences, nothing is quite as effective, personal, and engaging as a top executive—CEO, business owner, executive director, civic manager, or leader in volunteer community service—addressing public audiences online and in-person.

For many organizations, it also makes a positive difference if mid- or local-level managers engage in local community outreach as well. To facilitate this, it's often crucial for a top executive to show up to introduce and support local managers in the community. Engagement by local team members with the community builds public confidence, the effects of good sales and service, and your organization's overall development.

Motivated in part by a heartfelt kindness as well as shrewd responsibility, each of the exemplars noted in this book started out learning public speaking step by step, kept it as a priority, and found it helped them be effective leaders. You can as well—let this be you!

CHAPTER 43

Common Mistakes
in Giving a Public Speech

Years of experience in consulting with CEOs and other professionals about public speaking have identified key mistakes which leaders can
make...

...In Choosing a Topic

A first temptation for many is to get all caught up in "pitching" a message with "impact" instead of thinking about truly communicating with
the audience. Widely published communication theorist Dervin[1] referred
to this notion as "the message as a brick" syndrome, tossing a message out
there to make a big impression.

Instead, as emphasized in previous chapters, look into the specific
interests and concerns of the audience at the outset in setting up the topic
of your speech. Listen first. Consider where your listeners "are coming
from," their ways of thinking, key emotions, as well as elements crucial to
you, and then develop your message accordingly.

In exploring all this, reflect on their comments to adjust your material and to identify a best-fit title. If you are giving a series of talks to a
variety of groups, most likely you can give your material a unique twist to
fit each audience especially well.

...In Preparing to Speak

Clearly, it's risky to just "wing it" or put off your preparation until the
last minute. If you don't prepare carefully, you'll likely waste not only your
audience's time and attention, but also your organization's resources—and
damage your own reputation.

How far in advance should you prepare? Consider the Chairman and CEO who wanted to be out speaking three times a month. He insisted that each speech be written out in full and ready to go a month in advance. Is that realistic today in this era of texts and "the latest"? Maybe it can be— if you stay alert.

This top executive, later the head of one of the largest banks in the world, liked to be thinking about his speeches for a good while, letting his reflections percolate well in advance. He had a sharp eye for details, and he also kept on top of what was happening. For his speechwriter, nailing his key thoughts concisely, and then getting key updates to him in a timely way, wasn't easy.

Writing these speeches was quite a challenge because he tended to speak at a rate of 150 words per minute, instead of the average of 110 wpm. Our target was 17–18 minutes for the typical breakfast or luncheon speech. At his speed of delivery, that took a lot of writing.

Most important, however, was that he knew how to tune into an audience quickly and personalize his remarks and his delivery. It seemed natural. He by nature was kind and considerate, but he worked hard on all of this, and he was smart. He often started with thanking the introducer and adding a compliment. If appropriate, he would acknowledge one or two people he knew or had just met. It seemed he always had at least one acquaintance or two, at least a new one, in every audience he addressed.

Speaking regularly kept his skills sharp. He had built up strength in delivery, and by the time we worked together he could launch into every speech opportunity with minimal preparation—with skill and confidence. Maybe he was a genius and, like this author you're not, but you can martial your resources to be much more efficient than you think.

In your case, it may be best to shoot for having a good first draft in your hands at least two weeks in advance. This would be much easier on you than the incipient pangs of anxiety that arise a week ahead or less if you are not prepared. Early readiness also can allow you to develop additional, perhaps better thoughts, even a "big idea" you can apply in many ways.

...In Using a Script

No one wants to sit and watch a speaker reading a script word-for-word, with little contact with the audience. Dull, boring, dead on arrival. So does this mean memorize? No, not necessarily, unless you have a gift for total recall.

An experienced speaker can scan a script and then deliver it effectively "cold," referring to the script often but with good eye contact. This is an acquired skill, which means that with practice and "mileage" you can learn to do this. But don't push your luck. Make it your goal to at least get a good grasp of each major idea in your speech well in advance. Ask yourself questions, even kick these ideas around a bit with trusted associates, to nail—and remember—your thoughts clearly.

Be aware that at times there are particularly good reasons to be ready to deliver a script word-for-word. When addressing a sensitive topic, especially when media are present, in speaking to analysts, or at an annual meeting—if you value your career—be sure to avoid making comments that are careless or uninformed. In such situations use words carefully chosen; if you start to get ahead of yourself, slow down, pause, and proceed carefully.

Also, if you or a capable assistant can prepare a full text that is easy for you to stick to, after you review and approve it, your team could hand out advance copies to the media or other key observers—so you are not misquoted, and so your script can have a longer lifespan, perhaps in reprints or summarized online.

…In "Reading" Your Script

With good work and practice, you can learn how to read from a script with a natural flow of discourse. Actors learn to do this, but you can, too. A great help is to practice upcoming speeches with video as soon as you can—at least one "take" so you can look at yourself before the event. You'll immediately see ways to improve. But there's more to it than that.

One secret is that if someone prepares a final script for you, when you get it, read through it immediately. That sets the wheels of memory and delivery turning, so you're "started" when you have time to get back to work on the speech further.

Looking back, this author first learned to read aloud effectively by reading books to our children at bedtime when they were little (loved it, still miss it). Serving as a lector at public services can be another major help. Volunteering to read announcements and give reports at service-club or interest-group meetings can make a big difference. All this can open the door for you to be comfortable with notes and be able to read aloud skillfully with little preparation.

Script format counts. Set up your script in large, serif type (more easily readable than sans-serif), in a narrow column—not full-page width. A format this speechwriter favors—for scripts on paper—is using the 16 pt. Times New Roman font, in lines one-and-a-half spaced, and an approximately five-inch line length, with a wide margin on the left. Underline key words and phrases. Coach yourself a bit with margin sub-headings and short notes on the side.

Finally, leave the bottom third of each page blank, so you don't end up looking down to the bottom of the page, losing eye contact with the audience, leaving them "wondering where you went." In addition, instead of flipping the pages in a binder—which is annoying, unprofessional, and distracting, especially on-camera—slide them side-to-side, keeping them in order in a folder, for your reference later, including during Q&A.

As you put in such effort, your delivery with a script, any script, will get easier. You may not get to the skill level of a media professional, but close enough.

...In Making Contact

Don't underestimate the value of personal contact. Look at the audience. They want to see you. They want to hear you. If you are open, they want to get to know you, at least somewhat. See them, pay attention to them. If it's an online format, look for any and all clues on how the audience is reacting. It matters.

Again, the audience wants you to be successful—at least so they are not uncomfortable as they sit there, "stuck" with you, or wasting their time until their next appointment. So pick up on any positive vibes that may come your way. And be positive back.

...About a Sense of Service

Above all, keep in mind that the speech is not just about you, most especially it's about engaging with your audience, learning from their reactions and questions, and helping them deal with the topic at hand, particularly if it's something very concerning. In order to focus on the audience, a sense of service on our part—service to others—counts.

One suggestion for strengthening this is to envision yourself reaching out—over and beyond the lectern—to take the audience by the hand to walk down a road together, helping one another consider new ideas, deal with issues, and develop a sense of mutual trust. Such positive regard makes a difference!

...In Answering Questions

Even with a small audience, in taking questions at the end of a speech, at least in an in-person format, be sure to repeat the question so all can hear it. Some listeners may be hard of hearing. In-person, a questioner usually talks only to the speaker, often making it difficult for others on the sides and in the back to pick up the thought, the tone, and the intent of the question. Repeating the question also gives you time to think about a good response. Remember to keep your answers short, to give others time to be heard as well, and to give yourself a chance to learn more.

Seize the Opportunity

Effective public speaking takes effort; you need to do the work. Highly recommended is doing the work to master the basics early in your career when you have more time and face less pressure than later, at the executive level. Get help from a pro if and when you can. Seize good opportunities to improve your skills. You'll be glad you did as your career develops.

It's true that many good speakers are still nervous no matter what, but this author is convinced that practicing the skills noted above can help anyone get in the groove and do well. Once you do, you'll agree there's no better way to win a wide base of supporters, customers, and friends, and to influence a variety of people who are important to you and to your organization.

CHAPTER 44

Ten "Quick Tips" to Keep in Mind

Quick Tip 1: Plan Your Outreach

Instead of just responding to speech invitations that happen to come your way, your outreach as an executive should be based on strategic planning. How well does it work to rely only on chance in managing other aspects of your business?

In this era of divisiveness and un-resolved issues, as well as new initiatives in business and industry, now is the time to rebuild or strengthen relationships with the community with care, to identify vital speaking opportunities, and to make your mark as a skillful and effective leader.

How Often?

You don't have time to give speeches? A reasonable amount of public speaking is a powerful, unmatched way to build your business—and your success. Even a conservative speech-calendar "time budget" can make a big difference. For clients in several industries a reasonable interval for top-executive public speaking tends to be six to eight times a year. Consider that:

- Quarterly is not often enough to make progress in your speaking skills, to build continuity in your messaging, and to achieve an effective program of public outreach.
- Mid–January through May and September through mid–November are the prime times for addressing public forums. Get on top of the good opportunities.
- Financial reporting schedules can be a key variable in your calendar.
- For public speaking, you owe it to yourself and to your organization to develop a sensible outreach plan and get going to achieve worthwhile results.

About What?

For reaching out to community audiences, your speeches could cover a variety of topics. If you're a leader in a major enterprise, corporate or not-for-profit, you may have a communications team that has identified key "messages" or themes—in a public relations or marketing plan—to be covered in the current year. If so, work with a professional to set the theme, tone, and details of what your speech could cover.

In the long term, consider "big picture" work with your communications staff or outside help to: (1) identify worthwhile speech opportunities, (2) seek invitations for you from key forums, (3) help with speech development, and (4) arrange for further use of your remarks in public and company media.

If you're on your own, it's usually best to address a development in your industry that's in the news as a matter of general interest. You can include specific points about your own enterprise as examples, without trying too hard to "sell" your own business plan. Audiences may have thoughts, questions, feelings you'll encounter; at least you could get them started on a topic that is of mutual interest and well worth their attention—and yours.

Quick Tip 2: Consider Both In-Person and Virtual Speaking

Should you seek to speak to in-person or to online public forums? You may need to deal with both—you'll likely need to go with the format chosen by the forums that invite you. We've addressed traditional in-person speeches as well as online public speaking. Both are here to stay and both can provide outstanding opportunities.

Online formats using video conferencing technology may be the case for addressing audiences from small groups to major audiences at the local, national, and international levels. Yet in-person speaking is always a possibility for groups large and small, and it's a good way to master fundamentals.

Your Script—In-Person vs. Virtual

Instead of the standard 17–18 minutes for an in-person breakfast or luncheon address, for online delivery your material should be especially straightforward, short, and simple. You may be given less time, perhaps 10–15 minutes. Even a seven- to ten-minute range could be ideal depending on the dynamics of the online forum you are addressing.[1]

Key Rules for Virtual Forums

In advance of your event, make sure that you check how you look and how you sound online. Do at least one dry run on-camera, onsite. Test the microphone and check the lighting (especially on your face), the visible background (not too "busy"), your overall appearance, and the way you'll handle your notes (not too distracting). Be prepared to cover your key ideas in a timely way, and leave extra minutes for questions and interaction.

If you have your own video team with studio access, work with them well before the day of your event. If you think you can "do it yourself" with your own digital equipment, a computer might suffice, but look into buying a current-technology videocam, a high-quality mic, and additional light source(s). Practice well in advance and review how you look on-screen.

As you speak, be sure to look directly into the camera all the time. For a favorable appearance the camera should be at or slightly higher than your eye level. Keep the background simple but not barren. No inappropriate books, photos, or artwork. A few items indicating your personal "brand" could be perfect. No too-bright, glaring light sources, no backlighting (it darkens your face), no distracting shadows.

If you are not familiar with the technology, make sure to have someone stand by and be ready when you speak to help you fix things or switch to backup equipment if necessary.

Preparing for an In-Person Event

By all means, for a traditional in-person public speech do not overlook the need to prepare and to practice. Set up the format of your script for ease of eye contact and delivery, and consider how to stand and move at a lectern, and locate people in three different spots in the room to take turns looking at to vary your eye contact.

In advance, for in-person as well as online speeches, practice with video on your own turf to see and critique yourself—or with the help of a pro if possible. Experiment with how to stand with balance and ease, how to keep track of your notes, how to move with purpose if and when it makes sense, and how to connect with different sections of the audience.

Quick Tip 3: Give a "Speech," Not a Presentation

There's a fine line between what constitutes a speech as compared with a presentation. A business speech to a community audience is down-to-earth, informational, straightforward, and personal, relying on speaking "from the heart."

A presentation is information-intensive, offering data and visuals, sometimes flair, even some drama and visual imagery. Presentation visuals could include slides, social media, video clips, dramatic animation. Entertaining? Maybe, yet too often the visual elements are overdone, boring, and impersonal.

Nothing beats the leadership power of a down-to-earth, thoughtful, well-constructed, full-on eye contact, well-delivered, heartfelt speech. (Yes, you can include some slides, even some video in a speech, but they should only play a minor role.) A speech should especially be about connecting with the audience. In general, the ability to give such a speech effectively can be your best friend in leadership, and in particular for establishing longer-term community ties.

The good business speech seeks not to entertain or be a show, but to engage, inform, lead, and develop enduring relationships with your listeners.

It's About a Relationship

With a straightforward speech—in-person or online—you indeed can create a positive relationship with your audience. Audience members want to hear from you. They want to know what kind of a leader you are, and what makes you—and your organization—tick. It's personal!

In addition, consider that your best takeaway can be something you learn from them, through their reactions, their questions, their emotions, and their comments afterwards. Show that you are interested in them, and value the opportunity to learn more about them.

You'll find that heartfelt remarks along with good eye contact with your audience can be more rewarding than you ever might expect.

Quick Tip 4: Co-Question

Above all, as you speak to a public audience, your basic perspective can make all the difference. It's not just about you or about them. Put it all together.

Approach the opportunity not just to "tell them what you want to tell them," but with an open mind to listen to and learn from your audience as you get ready to speak, and as you take questions from them later, so that you and the audience probe your subject matter together. Develop your talk in this spirit of co-questioning, aided by research you do in advance at least with the program chair or event chair, and if possible with carefully-selected members of the audience.

In your audience research, make it about them, try to learn some of their relevant thoughts and feelings. You'll likely have a basic message you want to develop, yet begin to approach your audience with an intent to be responsive to their interests and their perceptions.

In a nutshell, *listen in advance* to a few of the people you will be addressing. Consider their personal situation, their perspective on you and your organization, their inquisitiveness, their experience, their concerns if any about you and what you might have to say.

You may be the expert, but even you can learn something from the audience at least from their questions. Plan for perhaps ten minutes at the end of your speech for what could be a lively and mutually beneficial question-and-answer period. Stay on for a couple of minutes later, after you're finished, to show you are interested.

This may seem like a tall order, but it really isn't so complicated. Don't just go there to "educate" them. Set a tone of collaboration and mutual respect, make it your goal to have everyone arrive at a new level of insight—together. If you go to speak with the audience's concerns in mind as well as your own, and if you also look to get at least one good idea from them, you all will learn something new.

And you'll be well on your way to a track record of worthwhile and successful public speaking.

Quick Tip 5: Be Structural

Fear of public speaking daunts us all, even experienced professionals. What's at least one good way to handle this? Your best bet is good speech structure—a foundation you can depend on for support and effectiveness. A classic approach is to set up a brief opening, a main theme (usually one sentence), and three major points relevant to your topic and your audience. The "one-two-three" sequence of major points is pleasing, easy to remember, and a framework that supports the heart of an effective message.

Present, Past, Future

One useful example could be to discuss an overall time frame, but with a twist: Present, Past, and Future. For the Present you could review current conditions related to your topic. Then turn to the Past for perspective, perhaps leading into it by saying, "Let me take you back...." As for the Future, you could construct a new solution and envision possible outcomes.

All this assumes that you'll position your three points between an effective opening and a summary-and-conclusion.

Parts One, Two, and Three

Another frame of reference for your three major points could be set your views in a sequence presented as "Chapter One, Chapter Two, and Chapter Three." An alternative that could work for you might be to discuss one extreme point of view, then the other, and finally the "sweet spot" in between. Or you could present a problem in some detail, then an approach that didn't work and why, and finally a promising, new solution that you advocate or have applied at your own enterprise.

The Point?

Varieties of three-element structures are boundless. Just be sure to keep the overall structure of your speech simple, strong, and easy to deliver, and you'll be OK. So will your audience.

Timing

A structural approach also helps you manage the speaking minutes you have available. You may have only a few precious minutes for an online talk. If you are giving an in-person, sit-down breakfast or luncheon speech, the ideal time frame may be 17–18 minutes. Online timing may be shorter, perhaps 15 minutes.

An in-person, formal dinner speech typically is somewhat longer, perhaps 25 minutes, and may require a fourth major point, or at least more examples, or stories.

A supposedly one-hour conference keynote speech usually runs approximately 35–37 minutes, including examples and time for visuals. This time-frame is a result of typical delays in starting, time for being introduced, and for questions at the end. An online conference keynote, however, may be limited to a shorter time frame. Even so, a training event may have specific speaking-time requirements, such as 50 minutes, for the listeners to get one hour of credit. It might be a good idea to have an additional major point (and scripting) you can add if need be.

In any case, if you keep your fundamental structure simple and evident, and develop the components carefully with good timing, your remarks will be well understood, effective, and memorable.

Quick Tip 6: Be Conversational

You're prepared, ready, and are being introduced. Whether you are speaking to an online audience or an in-person assembly, what can you do to help your talk feel "conversational"?

For an online audience, continued eye contact with the camera is essential (looking off-camera is distracting and dysfunctional). For an in-person speech, one suggestion is to select and focus on three individuals "out there" that you can see readily to address, one on your left perhaps near you, one on the right perhaps farther out, and one in the middle at the very back.

Choose a "friendly" face—someone you know, someone you'd like to meet, or someone who's particularly attentive to what you are saying. If you feel the eye contact is not working well for you, however, pick substitutes as you go. But don't get too distracted and overdo it.

As you speak, hold eye contact with each person for a few moments, at least long enough to express a complete thought—as in a conversation.

Vary Your Eye Contact

At an in-person forum, as you speak, develop eye contact naturally—not predictably—or you'll distract your listeners. You don't want them to start keeping score on how many times you mechanically look here or there. And don't pace back and forth. If conditions (microphone, staging, lighting) allow, you could change your standing position from one side of the lectern to the other for a short time as you transit from one major point to the next.

Too many speakers tend to speak mostly to one side of the audience, and too many don't consider those in the back. By the way, as you look to the back, slightly over the heads of your audience in front of you, most of the people in the foreground still will think you are looking directly at them! So, for the majority of the time, speaking to the back can be a good bet.

Give Yourself a Break

When you listen in advance and prepare to make good contact with your listeners, you'll worry less about yourself and become more relaxed. You'll be able to get into the spirit of inviting them to explore your topic with you, stir up their curiosity, share emotions, and introduce helpful ideas. They'll sense your genuine interest in them, they'll appreciate your efforts, and you'll like the results.

Quick Tip 7: Preview Your "Act"

As an executive-speech professional, it's clear to me that the single best tool to help you deliver a speech effectively—in-person or online—is to see yourself in advance on-screen in a practice session. Use a video camera or at least a smartphone while practicing. When you witness yourself giving a speech in advance, things are ripe for change.

Don't put this off to the last minute. Make doing so well in advance a priority.

Will you see bad habits, needs for improvement? Yes, everyone does. To cure them, go to work, like this:

- Do your practice if possible with a speech professional, or at least with a staff member or a friend—someone who can give you a reasonably objective point of view.
- For a first practice, if your new script isn't ready but you have a moment to work on delivery, speak from an old script at least for two or three minutes.
- After such a short segment, stop, and watch the video. If someone is with you, talk about your delivery. Identify bad habits. Make a few notes about ways to improve. Consider strong points to be able to accentuate the positive.
- Try it again, especially with your new script, for two or three more times if possible. Work on the skills you need to attain.
- Your goal should be continuous improvement.

The Actual

For when you actually deliver your speech, ask someone to make or get a video for your use later, perhaps with a smartphone. Review the video soon after the event. This is when you will learn the most about improving your delivery!

In addition, call the event chair a day or two after the event to ask for feedback about what you said, about your delivery, and ask informally if the person heard any comments about the speech, and if so, what. (This approach seems to be aptly non-threatening.)

For clients, as negotiated in advance, my work included getting feedback at least from the program or event chair, if not a couple others in addition, usually preliminary contacts I interviewed while researching the speech. The feedback interview included a few structured and open-ended questions on key points.

Does all of this sound like you're being too vain or self-absorbed? Although what counts the most is what you have to say, delivery can make all the difference. Do what it takes to learn to say it well—and be your best! You owe this to your audience, your team, and yourself.

A Caveat

In speaking to a public audience, your ability and reputation as a leader is on the line. Why not get professional help, why not early in your career? That could make a big difference. Work with professionals—a speech coach, a speechwriter, especially a speechwriter who also knows the ins and outs of effective delivery and can help you adjust your scripts as needed.

Having a fully qualified speech professional helping you from the get-go throughout the whole process makes practicing a disciplined matter, gets useful feedback, allows quick changes, and provides further guidance if and when you need it to make your upcoming speeches "right."

Quick Tip 8: Juke Your Second Major Point

So you've been introduced, delivered your opening and your theme statement, and are finishing your first major point. Audience members have tuned into you, are liking you, are following what you are saying, at least most everyone, and they're comfortable. No worries? Wrong!

The Danger Zone

In a flash, as you turn to your second major point, you easily could lose a big share of your audience. Why? Perhaps they're settling in a bit too well, having enjoyed the event's breakfast or lunch, or dinner. Especially after a luncheon, your listeners' internal clock may say it's time to kick back, take a mental break, and catch you later.

Be prepared.

Ready, Set, "Juke"

Be proactive! Like a soccer player or football running back, juke the audience. Take a turn for the better. Maybe add a brief, uplifting story leading into your second major point. Or ask a rhetorical question to set up what's next.

For an in-person speech, put a move on. Change your stance at the lectern. If you have a lavalier microphone, take a couple of steps to one side or the other.

Such techniques raise a subtle call to attention, introduce a note of surprise, and add extra energy. The point is to do something special to regain attention, affirm your line of thought, and "win."

Quick Tip 9: Identify What Works for You

The best way to know what works well for you, and to see if you are improving in public speaking, is to get structured feedback after the event. Have someone help you with this, if possible, each time you give a speech. Let the long-term patterns be your guide on weak points you need to deal with, and on making good use of skills that work especially well for you.

Questions to Ask

For useful feedback, let's consider at least one combination of quantitative and qualitative questions. An initial softball question to ask a program or event chair is, "Among speakers you've had lately, would you put that speech in the top third, middle third, or bottom third of such speeches?" (A little repetition of the word "speech" helps put the emphasis on the actual speech instead of the speaker.) And then ask, "Why?" Pause and listen for the person's response, and make a note of it. Sometimes it's difficult to pause instead of saying something more. Wait, and listen— even if it feels awkward for a moment.

Respondents typically are a bit too generous at first, so a good follow-up can be "By the numbers, on a scale where 0 = Very Poor, and 10 = Excellent, how would you rate the speech overall?" This helps get to the heart of the matter. Follow that with "What worked best?" Pause, listen for specifics, and make a note of each significant response.

Another productive question is, "What one story, concept, or idea seemed to be of particular interest to the audience?" This is especially useful for knowing what material to save and emphasize in future speeches.

Good Data

Such questions may not yield scientific accuracy. Yet my years of experience in getting feedback for dozens of CEOs and other leadership speakers have shown that these questions are constructive, don't take too long, and give you useful data you can trend over the long run. The program or event chair will appreciate your diligence, and respect your professionalism.

With steady and determined efforts to evaluate your efforts and develop your skills, you'll learn a lot about people and about yourself. And you'll definitely sharpen your ability to be an effective public speaker.

Quick Tip 10: Be Careful, Tell the Truth

If you're mindful of the preceding guidance, you'll be on your way to good public speaking. Even so, always bear in mind the following note of caution about what you say and how you say it.

In today's environment, any public talk you give, especially in an online format, even to a small, rather informal audience, could be taped at least in part, whether you know it or not, and end up online—and possibly go viral. In the past, professional communicators advised that what you say in an email, even a text message, could end up on the "front page" of the media. Any public speech you give—in-person or virtual—could be played online anywhere, any time.

So:

- Do not make negative, disparaging comments about your team members, whether they are other executives or the newest, junior member of your organization. Be positive, supportive.
- Don't mention internal politics or complain about the competition.
- Don't "wing it" on sensitive matters. At least prepare an outline, if not also write out word-for-word, for what you have to say about such topics. If you have communications staff to turn to, have them review your intentions, thoughts, and written material in advance.
- Be organized, be careful about your appearance; usually you'd want to look presidential.
- In general, take your act up a notch for the sake of your team.
- Most important: always tell the truth. It's easy to fluff around the edges. Be straightforward instead, and say it "right."

If all of this seems obvious, too often it's too easy to forget basics.

As mentioned in a previous chapter, the president of a major league team recently broke some of these rules. His speech to a small service club went viral—and shortly thereafter he got fired! A not-so-sharp appearance and careless comments—disrespect, conflicts, team politics—was a disaster for him and everyone concerned.

Above all—it should go without saying, but let's toughen up—truth wins out in the long run, the truth is your friend. Don't be misled by the apparent success of the lies and distortions of other leaders. Anything less than the truth could—and most likely will—come back to haunt you and your team, harm customers, impair investors, or cause damage in the community. Use good judgment.

CHAPTER 45

Use a Speechwriter?

Is it okay to use a speechwriter? This question can be relevant for most any chief executive—the head of any enterprise be it major corporate or not-for-profit, owners of well-established smaller businesses, professionals, independent consultants, and startups. This author has worked with all of these, sometimes with adjustments in the scale of my services (sticking to just a few basics, perhaps just for setting up a plan, or for developing an outline, or for editing a script).

In this perspective, speech preparation can become a division of labor. Preparing a well-constructed public speech with an enduring message may take from 20 to 50 hours of work, depending on the complexity of the topic and the pressure of the occasion. Few CEOs, at least in large enterprises, have the time, and perhaps the expertise, to do the job sufficiently themselves.

The Work

Good speech preparation requires a number of skilled activities, some evident and some not so obvious:

- Listening in advance by way of audience and topic research.
- Developing a sound underlying structure for the message.
- Careful laying out of key points and examples responsive to specific audience interests.
- Thoughtful selection of personal stories—perhaps including humor—that make a point effectively.
- Inclusion of key corporate policy messages that are top priorities for the company.
- And sharp writing and editing to get it all down to 17–18 minutes of remarks that are responsive, clear, and memorable, and open the door to further, mutual inquiry with audience members.

Do such skills along with efficient preparation come easily and quickly for a senior executive? Usually not. Should such a leader get help, from either a staff member or consultant? If the speech event is important enough for you to be there, if the future of your enterprise and of your career is on the line, the answer most likely should be "yes!"

Turn the Question Around

Well and good, but let's take all this to the next level—for your sake— and change the question. Is it worthwhile for you and your enterprise to get better at reaching out to public audiences in ways that you can learn best from a public speech professional?

It's no secret that turnover at the top has accelerated in recent years. CEOs come and go. There will be room if you are not there yet. If you are at the top, what do you need to be nimble enough to stay there?

Remember the value of public outreach and making a good impression on your stakeholders by way of public speaking. Find someone who can identify what you need, be content with a low profile, work with you to set goals for improving your speeches, choose worthwhile and challenging audiences, be versatile enough to help you with preparation, and foster effective delivery—online and in-person. If you find a match, stick with that person for a good while.

Trust, Reliability, Tact

Lucky is the top executive who can find someone to trust to do the homework and get things in synch. Lucky the company that has internal or dedicated external talent to help as needed. Lucky the dedicated speechwriter who gets to work with a good team.

Fortunate the company that can recognize and support all this and commit to working with a speech professional over a reasonably long term.

Managing the Speech Calendar

A key point is that along with preparing remarks should go the responsibility for the speech pro to manage the public speech calendar for the top executive, or possibly the C-Suite team. Big responsibilities? Pitfalls? Sensitivity? Need for good judgment? A careful, professional approach? Worth it? Yes, yes, yes, yes, yes, and yes.

Worth the Expense?

Let's look further at whether the speechwriter is worth the money. Part of the answer includes whether the company values engaging with public audiences face to face, online or in-person. How important to the client is it to gain desirable visibility, show responsiveness, and be seen as leaders in the public eye?

In dealing with your personal finances, would you rather work with a junior accountant or a CPA? For your speeches, would you choose a junior writer with little experience or would you rather work with someone with proven skills and a track record of success?

Quite relevant today is whether the lack of public engagement by top executives with public audiences is one of the reasons why we see more and more public hostility toward business. Let's leave that to critics to debate and scholars to explore.

In the meantime, in light of political pressure and social needs for increased taxation, consumer unrest, and activist protests, as well as unprecedented economic difficulties—developing positive relationships with community members of all kinds can make a big difference for you and your team. Healthy engagement with public groups through public speaking may need to be more of a priority for businesses large and small.

Fundamentally, as emphasized in these chapters, executive speeches are not just about "speaking," but also "listening"—to questions, complaints, requests, and suggestions. This author has seen executives come back from a speech with a new idea—sometimes "a big idea"—for improving relationships with the public, adding new market share, and increasing stakeholder satisfaction.

On the Cheap Is Not a Bargain

For a major company in the public eye, if the company shortcuts speech outreach and preparation and chooses to work only with an inexpensive beginner, such "bargains" can be trouble, or at least impair good opportunities.

How much is the top executive's time worth? If a pro can do the work, think like a CEO, and take your public outreach to a higher level, then the good speechwriter earns the money. How much? It would be best for you to have a conversation about that with top prospects about how well prepared they are, about their experience, about their dedication to public service, and about whether they can be available for a reasonable length of time.

A Fresh Pair of Eyes

Here's a related perspective one observer shared and might apply to your situation: if an upcoming speech is about a topic the speaker is familiar with, or speaks about routinely, there may be less need for outside help. Yet, on the flip side, there can be value in getting a fresh set of eyes to polish a routine presentation and keep it lively.

Getting the Job Done

To be clear, working with a full-time speechwriter may not be in your budget, particularly for a small company or a not-for-profit entity. One way this author learned to deal with this was to focus only on particular elements in the formula noted at the outset of this book: "getting the right person to speak to the right group about the right subject at the right time in the right way with the right results."

Sometimes it is good just to focus on "speaking in the right way," or even just to speak to the right group. Some of this author's clients with a low budget were best helped by my lining up dates for a few speeches a year, identifying desirable contacts and getting speech commitments (through what this author set up as a "CEO Speakers Bureau" for these clients).

In such circumstances, this speechwriter would meet with the speaker to get a sense of the thoughts the person had in mind and how they could be structured. The next step was to develop desirable speech invitations by calling on audience contacts throughout the region, asking the program chair some basic questions about the forum, their interests, their views—and listening carefully to what came up.

After receiving these findings, it was up to the speaker to take charge of writing and delivering the speech (including practicing in front of a volunteer). Even so, this author required—as a last step—gathering carefully structured feedback (a scorecard for "the right way") and reviewing that with the speaker to facilitate further placements.

Our goal was continuous improvement, and it worked, as we stayed within the pre-arranged budget. The hourly average was seven to nine hours per event on my part. We felt it was "a deal."

Appendix 1: A Sample (Redacted) Executive Community Speech Calendar

Scenario for Regional Executive Public Speaking to Community Audiences

Month/Time	Venue	Audience	Media	Notes _____
Year One				
Jan, Tues @Lunch	Major Metro Service Club	200–250	Possible	Eastside
Feb, Tues @Lunch	Large Nearby East Service Club	150	Possible	Biz leaders
March, Fri @Lunch	Metro Service Club	150	Possible	Biz leaders
April, Tues @Lunch	Midtown Service Club	60	No	Good reference
May, Fri. @7:30 a.m.	Forum for CEOs of Midsize Firms	30–40	No	Networking
June, Fri @Lunch	Major Service Club, adjacent state	120	Possible	Major forum
July, Thurs @ Lunch	Large Midstate Service Club	180	Possible	Major forum
Aug, Tues @7:15 a.m.	Morning Metro Service Club	40–50	No	For new exec
Sept, Mon @Lunch	North City Service Club	100	Possible	Mainstay club

Month/Time	Venue	Audience	Media	Notes _____
Year One				
Oct, monthly meeting	Major Chapter, State Soc. CPAs	30–40	No	Best such forum
Nov, Wed @Lunch	Nearby So. Metro Service Club	125	Possible	Largest in area
Dec, Fri @Lunch	Major University Service Club	75	No	Local mgr. intro
Year Two				
Jan, Thurs a.m.	South state Chamber Keynote	50–72	Yes	Media sponsor
Feb, Thurs @Lunch	Key Major south city Service Club	130	Possible	Mainstay club
Mar, Thurs @Lunch	Major Service Club	250	No	Poss. short prog.
April, Mon @Lunch	North Major Service Club	75	Possible	Traditional group
May, 1st Thurs @ Lunch	Medium North Chamber	40	Possible	Growth area

Appendix 2:
Questioning Tactics for Executive Speech Development

Consider thought patterns such as the following as options you can use to research in advance the key thoughts and interests of your audience, and then to devise the main points of your speech. Be aware that any one of these could be used as an over-arching strategy including two or more of these tactics in simple or complex combinations. These tools are meant to be quite adaptable to situations you are dealing with.

1. Checking: Seeing if information is correct, or if everyone is on track.

2. Clarifying: Focusing or sharpening a statement or an idea that is ill-defined, inexact, or poorly stated.

3. Confirming: Verifying that something is true, correct, valid, approved, going to happen or that someone is authentic or approved.

4. Debating: With a little preliminary audience research you may discover that your audience is quite divided on the subject matter. In your speech you could cover both points of view to see which side has more convincing evidence. You then could point out why you are convinced the option you favor is best. Or perhaps, if you dare, you could arrange a formal debate with a speaker representing a point of view you wish to dispute.

5. Decision-making (choosing among alternatives): This fits an audience caught up in choosing between two or more alternatives, with little time for deliberation. Your role could be to help the audience broaden their thinking, at least by helping them weigh the pros and cons of each alternative.

6. Depicting: Illustrating by presenting a drawing, photograph, or a video relating to what you are speaking about.

7. Discussing: Your upcoming audience may not be "trending" on your speech topic, but it would be good to know if your topic is something people are talking about quite a bit already. Perhaps they just want to hear more discussion rather than a "conclusion." It may be best for you and the program chair to set up a panel discussion instead of a one-presenter speech.

8. Envisioning: Foreseeing a "big picture" of what the future could be like, especially a new level of experience you intend to work toward.

9. Experimenting: Following or at least reviewing generally accepted

techniques for conducting and reporting scientific experiments about your subject matter.

10. Following: Following the advice of someone you know or from something you are reading. Your audience may want to follow the development of next-step technologies in your business, or they may simply want an update on what is happening right now. Or they may want to know what sources you recommend for keeping up in the future.

11. Forecasting: Projecting or specifying a future development or outcome.

12. Hypothesizing: This doesn't necessarily need to be as formal as conducting an experiment, but at least could involve trying to foresee the outcome of acting on the topic you are covering, so your audience can check it out. Your approach could draw on prior experience or new evidence, and develop a logical expectation about what might happen next.

13. Imagining: One of the unique powers of public speaking is the opportunity to invite the audience to imagine or visualize new ways of seeing and doing things, rising above the everyday humdrum and tired procedures that retard progress and new achievements.

14. Inspiring: Using credible sources, logic, relevant examples, and your successes to urge others into action.

15. Judging: Weighing the pros and cons of alternatives in order to do whatever seems the best. You may have a reputation for having good judgment, and your audience may want to hear how you evaluate evidence about a particular subject. Alternatively, you could include in your speech, with a rather small audience, some interactive time to ask members of the audience what they see as pros and as cons about a series of options regarding a particular topic.

16. Pointed Questioning: Asking specific questions about the situation, such as "who, what, when, and where." The questions "why" and "how" may be about basic facts, or may entail broader, more complicated inquiry. In any case, the audience may have some specific "questions" in mind, and you'd better be prepared to deal with them. It's fairly common, of course, for corporate PR department or an experienced speaker to write out questions and answers, and sometimes for a speaker to rehearse persuasive answers in detail. This may be crucial if a speech is to be covered by the media, or for an Annual Meeting speech. Try your best to anticipate the tough questions, and get ready to give responsive, pointed answers.

17. Praying: Identified in a survey of a church organization as a method of inquiry.[1]

18. Probing: Repeating or continuing the questioning; an example in market research is "Can you tell me more?"

19. Problem Solving: Identifying the subject matter as a problem and looking for a "solution" is a common way to frame a topic of interest. Your audience may see your topic as involving an urgent problem, or as a problem they recognize but just don't want to deal with yet. Getting a sense of this in advance could make all the difference in how you proceed and what you emphasize in your speech.

20. Reflecting: forming thoughts, ideas, or opinions, or aspirations; meditating; sometimes closely related to praying.

21. Remembering: This is a broader concept than just happenstance of memory. Too often we find ourselves ignoring lessons from the past, and in a group or organization there may be only spotty remembrances of past days, issues, and learnings. Helping an audience recall key information from experience can be a true service as well as a way of earning respect and understanding for your own point of view.

22. Screening: Knowing at least one characteristic of what is wanted, looking for something with this characteristic. The audience may be looking for a product with a particular attribute, and won't listen to much else until you deal with that point. Or, if you can get a sense of what the audience tends to be seeking in regard to a particular issue, you can focus on that one element—and nail it.

23. Searching: Knowing the best thing to do and waiting for the opportunity to do it. Perhaps you could give examples (stories) from your experience of how this can work, and your message could focus on patience.

24. Seeing Opportunity: Identifying a promising gap in current circumstances whereby new action could be successful.

25. Seeking: Actively looking for any means to deal with the topic, or at least just waiting to see what comes up regarding the topic.

26. Testing: The next step beyond identifying a new strategy, hypothesis, or service improvement is actually putting it to the test, getting empirical evidence to see if a new approach pans out. In your speech you could discuss pertinent research that the audience may not be aware of.

27. Thanking: In itself a matter of whom or what to thank, for what and when, and a manner of how to thank—comes up in a variety of ways in public speeches.

28. Trial and Error: Trying something to see if it would help. The audience may or may not realize they are too caught up in "hit and miss" thinking, or it may be time for them to try something you'd recommend and see how it works. If you do recommend "just trying" something, however, you'd better have a solid basis for your recommendation.

29. Visualizing: Creating a visual representation of what you are thinking.

30. Waiting: Marking time while something is bound to happen.

Note: The possibilities for additional questioning tactics are unlimited.[2]

Appendix 3:
How to Co-Question with
a Conference Chair

A colleague recently asked, "So how do you do 'co-questioning?'" The following example, related to some real-life experiences, may be different from what you might expect. It includes a sequence of questioning, and tries to help a speaker deliver subtle empathetic outreach.

The Challenge

The main concern in this scenario is whether the audience at an international architectural awards conference would "get" the unique emphasis of a client's creative work and achievements. Also concerning in this case is whether the logistics of using a given set of visuals would be convincing, and fit into a limited time slot in a daylong schedule involving listeners with high expectations.

Arguably this is about a presentation, not a speech. Even so, the point is not just about delivering a message or showing slides, the focus is on relating the speaker's refined, creative skill, and connecting with the sensitivities of a demanding, critical audience.

The goal here is to tune into an audience in advance, pick up on what the emphasis should be, get a sense of emotions involved, and fit carefully into the expectations of a competitive audience of top-level professionals.

Setting Up the Call

Since the "speech pro" in this case is called in to help the client and his team refine a given set of material, the first step is to go through the client's visuals and tentative remarks, viewing the slides the team had already put together, and looking for the intended emphasis of what the client wanted to say, as well as the intended "feel" and pertinence of the slides.

After some discussion, the next step would be for the speech pro to set up a quick list of key questions to ask the conference's executive director. The intent here is to look for thought patterns, sensitivities, and points of emphasis that could carry the day most effectively on a level befitting a top award winner.

The Interview Guide

1. Why did this awards conference executive choose this design project, the paper submitted and the designed materials?
2. Why this topic?
3. Any similar topics at the conference?
4. Past presentations on this subject matter?
5. Anything particularly appealing in this professional's approach?
6. Anything strike you as unusual about the resulting work?
7. Your expectations about the talk, timing, use of visuals?
8. Anything else?

Note: While this interview guide was brief, for the busy executive director it was meant to get to the heart of the matter quickly. In using such a guide, it may help to intersperse probes like "Anything else?" and "Can you tell me more?"

The Interview Responses

The following comments, edited somewhat, are meant to keep the identity of the interviewee, the occasion, some key words, and the people involved confidential. This person, a seasoned professional, was quite responsive:

1. "His emphasis is so much on people, how people use public spaces."

   - "Most such architectural designers don't talk that much about people; I was impressed by that aspect of the proposal."
   - "The proposal was especially about children, and the diversity of people that use public spaces and the built environment as part of their quality of life."
   - "It was about joyful spaces, allowing people to get together and children to play in the sight of adults."

2. "The topic is important."

   - "The speaker will be in a plenary session, the last in the morning."
   - "This will be coming off of presentations we will want everyone to see: top award-winners."
   - "The afternoon presentations will be more scientific."
   - "Just before this individual is called up, there'll be a talk on 'social connectedness.'"
   - "I was very taken by one of his long-time projects in [a major city on the West Coast]."
   - "In this project this presenter was very perceptive about the relationship between social space and the built environment."
   - "This should not be a presentation about this winner's company. The conference is not really a medium for promotion of firms, but the presentation can illustrate ideas with his firm's work."

3. "As for other presentations," the executive director said, "there is overlap, in part. Most people believe in this kind of public space."

- "In the afternoon talks—about a country abroad, and then a local city—the topics are more specific, a little more research-oriented, not so open as this one."
- "Also, the next day there's a talk on the importance of child-friendly, child-active life."
- "Nothing is as *visionary* as this case."

4. "We haven't had anything like this in the past."
5. "Particularly appealing is his emphasis on children, elderly, and youth."

   - "It would be good to talk also about the elderly—and the diversity of ethnic groups, socio-economic diversity."
   - "It's healthy, equitable to take pleasure in each other's presence; and if there is diversity of ethnic foods to go with it, people like ethnic foods."

6. "What's unusual is his overall vision."

   - "It comes across clearly—how children and adults can have a good time together in a public space."

7. Expectations for logistics were:

   - "The talk should be 20–25 minutes, with 5–10 minutes of questions."
   - "If you do provide an introduction in advance, all the better."
   - "We expect the audience for this session to be approx. 300–350 people."
   - "On visuals, not too much text; images, minimal text."
   - "We have all the equipment; he can provide the presentation on a stick [jump drive], we would like it first thing that morning, even the day before to upload it."
   - "We would want a slide format that is compatible—be sure to check with the producer on compatibility."

8. When asked at the end about "anything else":

   - "The attendees will be very diverse: professionals, public health officials, elected officials."
   - "All will be in English."
   - "The speaker should bring materials about his firm."

The Result

After the interview, the point was to meet with the client and the staff, recap the interview, and go through the slides with them to make sure the emphasis was correct. We took out anything unnecessary, and made sure the client's remarks covered all of the key points indicated in the interview.

In the end, the executive director and the client were well pleased.

Chapter Notes

Preface

1. See Edelman's annual Trust Barometer, https://www.edelman.com.

Chapter 1

1. Stamm, K. (June 26, August 6, 2001). Personal communication. The need for a new paradigm was first posited by Carter, R. (1964). A Paradigmatic view of attitudes—An essay on orientation, coorientation, and communicatory behavior. Unpublished manuscript, Stanford Institute for Communication Research, Stanford.

2. To be explicated in detail in Chapter 7, this term was introduced in Kim, H-S. (2011). Climate change, science and community. *Public Understanding of Science*, 21(3), 268–285. https://doi.org/10.1177/0963662511421711.

3. Newcomb, T. (1953). An approach to the study of communicative acts. *Psychological Review*, 60(6), 393–404. https://doi.org/10.1037/h0063098.

4. Carter, R. (1966). Cognitive discrepancies and communication behavior. Paper presented to Association for Education in Journalism Communication, Theory and Methodology Division, Iowa City, Iowa.

5. Chaffee, S., & McLeod, J. (1968). Sensitization in panel design: A coorientational experiment. *Journalism Quarterly*, 45, 661–69. https://doi.org/10.1177/107769906804500406.

6. For example, Grunig, J., & Stamm, K. (1973). Communication and coorientation of collectivities. *American Behavioral Scientist* 16(4), 567–591. https://doi.org/10.1177/000276427301600407.

7. Stamm, K., & Pearce, W. (1971). Communication behavior and coorientational relations. *Journal of Communication*, 21(3), 198–309. https://doi.org/10.1111/j.1460-2466.1971.tb00919.x.

8. K. Stamm. (October 21, 2021). Personal communication.

Chapter 2

1. Politico. (September 1, 2020). https://www.politico.com/playbook.

2. Ted Leonhardt. (April 9, 2023). Personal communication.

Chapter 3

1. Crampton, C. (2020). The really, really short podcast. Hotpodnews.com, No. 257, May 5. https://hotpodnews.com/the-really-really-short-podcast.

2. Knox, B. (February 2, 2021). Personal communication.

3. Shaffer, M. (March 2, 2021). Personal communication.

4. Shaffer, M. (March 2, 2021). Personal communication.

Chapter 6

1. Weis, R. (1982). Questioning in a community. Unpublished doctoral dissertation, Univ. of Washington, 13–16.

Chapter 8

1. Carter, R. (1978a). Insure with the Eureka Holding and Assurance Company. Unpublished paper, School of Communications, Univ. of Washington; also online,

Behavioral Foundations of Effective Problem Solving. http://bfeps.org.

2. On an applied level, similar but unscientific terminology ("observe, judge, & act") was characteristic of the U.S. Young Christian Students organization, 1944–1980. Young Christian Students Records (YCS), University of Notre Dame Archives (UNDA), Notre Dame, IN 46556. https://archives.nd.edu/findaids/ead/xml/ycs.xml.

3. Carter, R. (1978b). A very peculiar horse race. In Bishop, G., Meadow, R., Jackson-Beeck, M. (eds.). *The presidential debates: Media, electoral and policy perspectives*, 3–17. Praeger.

4. Weis, R. (2003). A generous mentor and advisor, in Dervin, B., & Chaffee, S., with Foreman-Wernet, L. (eds.). *Communication, a different kind of horse race: Essays honoring Richard F. Carter*, 319. Hampton Press.

5. Chaffe, S., & McLeod, J. (1973). Interpersonal approaches to communication research. *American Behavioral Scientist*, 16:4, 469–99. https://doi.org/10.1177/000276427301600402.

6. Weis, R. (1982). Questioning in a community. Unpublished doctoral dissertation. Univ. of Washington.

7. Brouk, T. (2018). To give a great presentation, distill your message to just 15 words, Harvard Business Review online, Nov. 7, 2018. hbr.org.

6. Decety, J. (2020). Empathy in medicine: What it is, and how much we really need it. *Am. J. Med.*, May, 133 (5), 561–566. https://doi.org/10.1016/j.amjmed.2019.12.012.

7. King, W., & Mitchell, B. (2021). *Leadership matters*, 21. John Hopkins.

8. Cameron, C., Hutcherson, C., Ferguson, A., Scheffer, J., Hadjiandreou, E., & Inzlicht, M. (2019). Empathy is hard work: People choose to avoid empathy because of its cognitive costs. *Journal of Experimental Psychology*: General, Online First Publication, April 18. http://dx.doi.org/10.1037/xge0000595.

9. Aristotle. Roberts, R., transl. Solmsen, F., ed. (1954). *The rhetoric and the poetics of Aristotle*, xi. Simon & Schuster.

10. Plutchik, R. (1980). A general psychoevolutionary theory of emotion. In Plutchik, R., & Kellerman, H. (eds.), *Emotion: Theory, research and experience. Theories of Emotion* 1: 3–33. https://doi.org/10.1016/B978-0-12-558701-3.50007-7.

11. Cowen, A., & Keltner, D. (2017), Self-report captures 27 distinct categories of emotion bridged by continuous gradients. *PNAIS*, 114 (38a). https://doi.org/10.1073/pnas.1702247114.

12. Brouk, T. (2018). To give a great presentation, distill your message to just 15 words, Harvard Business Review online, Nov. 7. hbr.org.

Chapter 9

1. Goleman, D. (1995). *Emotional intelligence*. Bantam Books.

2. See Mayer, J., Caruso, D., & Salovey, P. (1999). Emotional intelligence meets traditional standards for an intelligence. *Intelligence*, 27, 267–298. https://doi.org/10.1016/S0160-2896(99)00016-1.

3. For example, see Connors, C. (2020). *Emotional intelligence for the modern leader: A guide to cultivating effective leadership and organizations.*

4. Aristotle. Roberts, R., transl. Solmsen, F., ed. (1954). *The rhetoric and the poetics of Aristotle*, 7. Random House.

5. Decety, J., & Cowell, J. (2014). Friends or foes: Is empathy necessary for moral behavior? *Perspectives on Psychological Science*, 9, 525–537. http://doi.org/10.1177/1745691614545130.

Chapter 11

1. Stamm, K. (June 21, 2021). Personal communication.

Chapter 12

1. Kim, H-S. (2020). Realizing interdisciplinarity among science, humanism, and art: A new paradigmatic explication of community problem solving. *Asian Communication Research*, 17(3), 20–54. https://doi.org/10.20879/acr.2020.17.3.20.

2. Kucera, V. (2019). Personal communication.

3. Chernow, R. (2004). *Alexander Hamilton*, 250. Penguin.

Chapter 13

1. Donald, D. (1995). *Lincoln*, 52. Cape.
2. Goodwin, D. (2005). *Team of rivals: The political genius of Abraham Lincoln*, 166. Simon & Schuster.
3. Goodwin, D. (2005). *Team of rivals: The political genius of Abraham Lincoln*, 259.

Chapter 14

1. Campbell, P. (February 14, 2022). Personal interview.

Chapter 15

1. Leonhardt, T. (December 29, 2021). Personal interview.

Chapter 16

1. Mitrovich, G. (2010). Rules for public speaking. *HuffPost*, Mar. 18. https://www.huffpost.com/entry/rules-for-public-speaking_b_337756.

Chapter 17

1. Aristotle. Roberts, R., transl. Solmsen, F., ed. (1954). *The rhetoric and the poetics of Aristotle*, 167. Random House.
2. Donald, D. (1995). *Lincoln*, 41. Cape.
3. Reynolds, D. (2020). *Abe*, 837; quoting Warren, L.A. (1974). *Lincoln's Gettysburg declaration: A new birth of freedom*. National Life Foundation, Ft. Wayne, IN, 54.
4. Reynolds, D. (2020). *Abe*, 586. Penguin.
5. Hulteng, J. (1974). Editorial writing (in-class, J564, U. of Oregon).
6. Miller, G.A. (1994). The magical number seven, plus or minus two: Some limits on our capacity for processing information. *Psychological Review*, 101(2), 343–352. https://doi.org/10.1037/0033-295X.101.2.343.

Chapter 18

1. Display, University of Washington's Burke Museum of Natural History and Culture.

Chapter 23

1. Aristotle. Roberts, R., transl. Solmsen, F., ed. (1954). *The rhetoric and the poetics of Aristotle*, 3. Random House.
2. Aristotle. Roberts, R., transl. Solmsen, F., ed. (1954). *The rhetoric and the poetics of Aristotle*, 6. Random House.
3. Aristotle. Roberts, R., transl. Solmsen, F., ed. (1954). *The rhetoric and the poetics of Aristotle*, 3. Random House.
4. Aristotle. Roberts, R., transl. Solmsen, F., ed. (1954). *The rhetoric and the poetics of Aristotle*, 8. Random House.
5. Aristotle. Roberts, R., transl. Solmsen, F., ed. (1954). *The rhetoric and the poetics of Aristotle*, 92. Random House.
6. Cicero, M. Hubbell, H., transl. (1993). *De inventione: De optimo genere oratorum*, 19–21. Harvard Univ. Press.
7. English Wikipedia (April 28, 2021). https://en.wikipedia.org/wiki/Confucius.
8. Liqing, Q., & Shangchao, M. (2009). A study on Confucius' views on language functions. *Polyglossia*, 16, 73. https://www.apu.ac.jp/rcaps/uploads/fckeditor/publications/polyglossia/Polyglossia_V16_Qiao_Min.

Chapter 24

1. Aristotle. Roberts, R. transl. Solmsen, F., ed. (1954). *The rhetoric and the poetics of Aristotle*, 7. Random House.

Chapter 26

1. Kim, H-S. (2003). A theoretical explication of collective life: Coorienting and communicating. In Dervin, B., & Chaffee, S. (eds.), *Communication, a different kind of horserace: Essays Honoring Richard F. Carter*, 117–134.

Chapter 27

1. Available from Brewer-Cantelmo Co., Inc., 109 W. 27th Street, New York, NY 10001.

Chapter 28

1. Carter, R. (Date not noted.) Personal communication.

Chapter 30

1. Kim, H-S. (2021). Realizing interdisciplinarity among science, humanism, and art: A new paradigmatic explication of community problem solving. *Asian Communication Research*, 17(3), 20–54. https://doi.org/10.20879/acr.2020.17.3.20.

Chapter 33

1. Putnam, R., with Garrett, S.R. (2020). *The upswing: How America came together a century ago and how we can do it again*, 285–286. Simon & Schuster.
2. Putnam, R., with Garrett, S.R. (2020). *The upswing: How America came together a century ago and how we can do it again*, 339. Simon & Schuster.
3. Putnam, R., with Garrett, S.R. (2020). *The upswing: How America came together a century ago and how we can do it again*, 183. Simon & Schuster.
4. Stamm, K. (1985). *Newspaper use and community ties*. Ablex.
5. Janowitz, M. (1952). *The community press in an urban setting*. Free Press.
6. Hillery, G. (1955). Definitions of community: areas of agreement. *Rural Sociology* 20: 111–123. http://www.hepg.org/her/abstract, 248.
7. Hillery, G. (1959). A critique of selected community concepts. *Social Forces* 36: 237–242.
8. Weis, R. (1982). Questioning in a community. Unpublished doctoral dissertation. Univ. of Washington.
9. Stamm, K., & Fortini-Campbell, L. (1983). The relationship of community ties to newspaper subscribing and use. *Journalism Monographs*, No. 84.
10. Stamm, K., & Fortini-Campbell, L. (1983). The relationship of community ties to newspaper subscribing and use. *Journalism Monographs*, No. 84, 13.
11. Stamm, K., & Fortini-Campbell, L. (1983). The relationship of community ties to newspaper subscribing and use. *Journalism Monographs*, No. 84, 20.
12. Carter, R. (1973). Communication as behavior, presented to Theory and Methodology Division. Association for Education in Journalism, Fort Collins, CO, 1973.
13. K. Stamm, (1985). *Newspaper use and community ties*, 32. Ablex.

Chapter 35

1. Weis, R. (2019a). Speech Doctor No. 30: What program chairs look for. Private email to clients of Weis Communications, Feb. 27.

Chapter 37

1. Weis, R. (2019b). Speech Doctor No. 31: What program conference organizers look for. Private email to clients, Weis Communications, Mar. 18.

Chapter 38

1. Douglas, D. (2014). Personal communication reprinted with permission. First published in Weis, R. (2019c). Speech Doctor No. 40: Serving on a panel. Private email to clients, Weis Communications, July 8.

Chapter 39

1. Williams, H. (2019). Personal communication reprinted with permission. First published in Weis, R. (2019d). Speech Doctor No. 41: Another perspective on panels. Private email to clients, Weis Communications, July 15.

Chapter 43

1. Dervin, B. (1976a). Graduate seminar, University of Washington; also see Foreman-Wernet, L. (2003). *Sense-making methodology reader: Selected writings of Brenda Dervin*. Hampton Press.

Chapter 44

1. See Obama, B. (2020). Graduate together: America honors the high school class of 2020, CNN online, commencement address, May 16.

Appendix 2

1. Weis, R. (1982). Questioning in a community. Unpublished doctoral dissertation. Univ. of Washington.
2. Carter, R. (1982). Personal communication.

Bibliography

Alexander, F., & Nelson, L. (1949). Rural social organization in Goodhue County, Minnesota. *U. of Minnesota Agr. Exp. Sta. Bull. No.* 401.

Aristotle. Roberts, R., transl. Solmsen, F., ed. (1954). *The rhetoric and the poetics of Aristotle.* Random House.

Baym, N. (1955). The emergence of community in computer-mediated communications. In Jones, S.G. (ed.), *Cybersociety: Computer-mediated communication and community.* Sage, 138–63.

Berelson, F., & Steiner, G. (1964). *Human behavior: An inventory of scientific findings.* Harcourt Brace.

Blumer, J., & Katz, E., eds. (1974). *Sage Annual Reviews of Communication Research, 3.*

Boczkowski, P. (1999). Mutual shaping of users and technologies in a national virtual community. *Journals of Communication,* 49(2), 86–108. https://doi.org/10.1111/j.1460-2466.1999.tb02795.x.

Bronowski, J. (1973). *The ascent of man.* Little, Brown.

Broom, L., & Selznick, P. (1973). *Sociology* (Harper & Row).

Brouk, T. (2018). To give a great presentation, distill your message to just 15 words. *Harvard Business Review* online, Nov. 7. hbr.org.

Bruner, J. (1973). *Beyond the information given.* W.W. Norton.

Cameron, C., Hutcherson, C., Ferguson, A., Scheffer, J., Hadjiandreou, E., & Inzlicht, M. (2019). Empathy is hard work: People choose to avoid empathy because of its cognitive costs. *Journal of Experimental Psychology:* General, Online First Publication, April 18. http://dx.doi.org/10.1037/xge0000595.

Carter, R. (1964). A paradigmatic view of attitudes—An essay on orientation, coorientation, and communicatory behavior. Unpublished manuscript, Stanford Institute for Communication Research, Stanford.

Carter, R. (1966). Cognitive discrepancies and communication behavior. Paper presented to Association for Education in Journalism Communication, Theory and Methodology Division, Iowa City, IA.

Carter, R. (1972). A journalistic view of communication. Paper presented to Association for Education in Journalism convention, Carbondale, IL.

Carter, R. (1973). Communication as behavior. Presented to Theory and Methodology Division. Association for Education in Journalism, Fort Collins, CO.

Carter, R. (1974a). Insure with the Eureka Holding and Assurance Co. Unpublished paper, School of Communications, Univ. of Washington.

Carter, R. (1974b). A journalistic cybernetic. Paper presented at the Conference on Communication and Control in Social Processes, Univ. of Pennsylvania, Annenberg School of Communication.

Carter, R. (1974c). Toward more unity in science. Unpublished paper, School of Communications, Univ. of Washington.

Carter, R. (1975). Elementary ideas of systems applied to problem-solving strategies. Paper presented at Far West Region of the Society for General Systems Research, San Jose.

Carter, R. (1977). Theory for researchers. Paper presented to Association for Education in Journalism convention, Madison, WI.

Carter, R. (1978a). Insure with the Eureka Holding and Assurance Company. Unpublished paper, School of Communications, Univ. of Washington; also online, Behavioral Foundations of Effective Problem Solving. http://bfeps.org.

Carter, R. (1978b). A very peculiar horse race. In Bishop, G., Meadow, R., & Jackson-Beeck, M. (eds.), *The presidential debates: Media, electoral and policy perspectives.* Praeger, 3–17.

Carter, R. (1980). Discontinuity and communication. Paper presented at Seminar on Communication from Eastern and Western Perspectives, East-West Communication Institute, East-West Center, Honolulu, HI.

Carter, R. (2022). https://bfeps.org (much of Carter's above material is restated or developed further here).

Chaffe, S., & Choe, S.Y. (1980). Newspaper reading in longitudinal perspective: Beyond structural explanations. Paper presented to Theory & Methodology Division, Association for Education in Journalism convention, Boston.

Chaffe, S., & McLeod, J. (1973). Interpersonal approaches to communication research. *American Behavioral Scientist,* 16:4, 469–99. https://doi.org/10.1177/000276427301600 402.

Chaffee, S., & McLeod, J. (1968). Sensitization in panel design: A coorientational experiment. *Journalism Quarterly,* 45, 661–69. https://doi.org/10.1177/107769906804500406.

Chernow, R. (2004). *Alexander Hamilton.* Penguin.

Cicero, M. Transl. Hubbell, H. (1993). *De inventione: De optimo genere oratorum.* Harvard University Press.

Connors, C. (2020). *Emotional intelligence for the modern leader: A guide to cultivating effective leadership and organizations.* Rockridge Press.

Cowen, A., & Keltner, D. (2017). Self-report captures 27 distinct categories of emotion bridged by continuous gradients, *PNAIS,* 114 (38a). https://doi.org/10.1073/pnas.1702247114.

Cox, H. (1965). *The secular city: Secularization and urbanization in theological perspective.* Macmillan.

Crampton, C. (2020). The really, really short podcast. Hotpodnews.com, No. 257, May 5. https://hotpodnews.com/the-really-really-short-podcast.

Decety, J. (2020). Empathy in medicine: What it is, and how much we really need it. *Am. J. Med.,* May 133 (5), 561–66. https://doi.org/10.1016/j.amjmed.2019.12.012.

Decety, J., & Cowell, J. (2014). Friends or foes: Is empathy necessary for moral behavior? *Perspectives on Psychological Science,* 9, 525–37. http://doi.org/10.1177/1745691614545130.

Dervin, B. (1976a). Graduate seminar, Univ. of Washington; also see Foreman-Wernet, L. (2003). *Sense-making methodology Reader: Selected writings of Brenda Dervin.* Hampton Press.

Dervin, B. (1976b). Information and sense-making. Paper presented to Symposium of the Committee on Public Information for the Prevention of Occupational Cancer, National Research Council, National Academy of Sciences.

Dervin, B. (1980a). Information as a user construct: The relevance of perceived information needs to synthesis and interpretation. Paper prepared for Research and Educational Practice Unit, National Institute for Education.

Dervin, B. (1980b). Sense-making handouts. Unpublished paper, School of Communications, Univ. of Washington.

Dervin, B. (1981). Communication gaps and inequities: Moving toward a reconceptualization, in Dervin, B., & Voight, M. (eds.), *Progress in Communication Sciences.* Ablex, 2.

Dewey, J. (1938). *Logic: The theory of inquiry* (H. Holt).

Donald, D. (1995). *Lincoln.* Jonathan Cape.

Donohew, G., et al. (1975). Mass media and the knowledge gap: A hypothesis reconsidered. *Communication Research,* 2:3–23. http://dx.doi.org/10.1177/009365027500200101.

Douglas, D. (2019). Pers. communication reprinted with permission, published in R. Weis Speech Doctor' No. 40: Serving on a Panel; private email to clients, Weis Communications, July 8.

Follet, M. (1919). Community is a process. *Philosophical Review,* 28:576–78. https://www. jstor.org/stable/2178307.

Gates, M. French. (2019). *The moment of lift: How empowering women changes the world.* FlatIron Books.

Goleman, D. (1995). *Emotional intelligence.* Bantam.

Goodwin, D. (2005). *Team of rivals: The political genius of Abraham Lincoln.* Simon & Schuster.

Goody, J., ed. (1978) *Questions and politeness: Strategies in social interaction.* Cambridge University Press.

Grunig, J. (1976). A progress report on multi-systems communication behavior. Paper presented at the Association for Education in Journalism convention (College Park, MD).

Grunig, J. (1978). Accuracy of communication from an external public to employees in a formal organization. *Human Communication Research,* 5:40–53. https://doi.org/10.1111/ j.1468-2958.1978.tb00621.x.

Grunig, J. (1979). Cognitive strategies and the resolution of environmental issues: A second study. *Journalism Quarterly,* 56:715–26. 10.1177/107769907905600403.

Grunig, J., & Stamm, K. (1973). Communication and coorientation of collectivities. *American Behavioral Scientist,* 16(4), 567–91. https://doi.org/10.1177/000276427301600407.

Grunig, J.E. (1975). A multi-systems theory of organizational communication. *Communication Research,* 2(2), 99–136. https://doi.org10.1177/009365027500200201.

Hillery, G. (1955). Definitions of community: Areas of agreement. *Rural Sociology,* 20:111–23. http://www.hepg.org/her/abstract/248.

Hillery, G. (1959). A critique of selected community concepts. *Social Forces,* 36:237–42. https://doi.org/10.2307/2572969.

Hillery, G. (1961). The folk village: A comparative analysis. *Rural Sociology,* 26:335–53.

Hillery, G. (1963). Villages, cities and total institutions. *American Sociological Review,* 28:779–91.

Hulteng, J. (1974). Editorial writing (Journalism Graduate Seminar, J564), U. of Oregon.

Janowitz, M. (1952). *The community press in an urban setting.* Free Press.

Jones, S.G. (1995). Understanding community in the information age. In Jones, S.G. (ed.), *Cybersociety: Computer-mediated communications and community.* Sage.

Kaplan, A. (1964). *The conduct of inquiry: Methodology for behavioral science* (Chandler).

Kerlinger, F. (1973). *Foundations of behavioral research,* second edition. Holt, Rinehart & Winston.

Kim, H-S. (2003). A Theoretical explication of collective life: Coorienting and communicating. In Dervin, B., & Chaffee, S. (eds.), *Communication, a different kind of horserace: Essays honoring Richard F. Carter.* Hampton Press, 117–134.

Kim, H-S. (2011). Climate change, science and community. *Public Understanding of Science,* 21(3), 268–85. https://doi.org/10.1177/0963662511421711.

Kim, H-S. (2020). Realizing interdisciplinarity among science, humanism, and art: A new paradigmatic explication of community problem solving. *Asian Communication Research* (17, 3), 20–54. https://doi.org/10.20879/acr.2020.17.3.20.

King, W., & Mitchell, B. (2021). *Leadership matters.* Johns Hopkins University Press.

Liqing, Q., & Shangchao, M. (2009). A study on Confucius' views on language functions. *Polyglossia,* 16. https://www.apu.ac.jp/rcaps/uploads/fckeditor/publications/polyglossia/ Polyglossia_V16_Qiao_Min.

Mayer, J., Caruso, D., & Salovey, P. (1999). Emotional intelligence meets traditional standards for an intelligence. *Intelligence* 27, 267–298. https://doi.org/10.1016/S0160-2896(99)00016-1.

Mayer, J., Caruso, D., & Salovey, P. (2016). The ability model of emotional intelligence: Principles and updates. *Emotion Review,* 8:1–11. http://dx.doi.org/10.1037/xge0000595.

Merton, R. (1950). Patterns of influence: A study of interpersonal influence and of communications behavior in a local community. In Lazarsfeld, P., & Stanton, F., (eds.), *Communications Research* 1948–49.

Miller, G. (1994). The magical number seven, plus or minus two: Some limits on our capacity for processing information. *Psychological Review,* 101(2), 343–52. https://doi. org/10.1037/0033-295X.101.2.343.

Mitrovich, G. (2010). Rules for public speaking. HuffPost, Mar. 18. https://www.huffpost.com/entry/rules-for-public-speaking_b_337756.

Munch, P., & Campbell, R. (1963). Interaction and collective identification in a rural community. *Rural Sociology*. Houghton Mifflin.

Newcomb, T. (1953). An approach to the study of communicative acts. *Psychological Review*, 60(6), 393–404. https://doi.org/10.1037/h0063098.

Obama, B. (2020). Graduate together: America honors the high school class of 2020, CNN online commencement address, May 16. https://www.nytimes.com › 2020/05/16 › us › obama-gra.

Plutchik, R. (1980). A general psychoevolutionary theory of emotion. In Plutchik, R., & Kellerman, H. (eds.), *Emotion: Theory, research and experience, theories of emotion* 1: 3–33). https://doi.org/10.1016/B978-0-12-558701-3.50007-7.

Putnam, R., with Garrett, S.R. (2020). *The upswing: How America came together a century ago and how we can do it again*. Simon & Schuster.

Reingold, H. (1993). *The virtual community: Homesteading in the electronic frontier*. Addison-Wesley.

Reynolds, D. (2020). *Abraham Lincoln in His Time*. Penguin.

Riess, H. (2018). *The empathy effect: Seven neuroscience-based keys for transforming the way we live, love, work, and connect across differences*. Sound True.

Riess, H., Kelley, J., Bailey, R., Dunn, E. & Phillips, M. (2012). Empathy training for resident physicians: A randomized controlled trial of a neuroscience-informed curriculum. *J Gen Intern Med* (10): 1280–86. doi: 10.1007/s11606-012-2063-z.

Rothenbuhler, E., Mullen, L., DeLaurell, T., & Ryu, C. (1996). Communication and community attachment and involvement. *Journalism and Mass Communication Quarterly*, 73(2), 445–66.

Shepherd, G., & Rothenbuhler, E. (2001). *Communication and community*. Erlbaum.

Stamm, K. (1985). *Newspaper use and community ties: Toward a dynamic theory*. Ablex.

Stamm, K., & Pearce, W. (1971). Communication behavior and coorientational relations. *Journal of Communication,* 21(3), 198–309. https://doi.org/10.1111/j.1460-2466.1971.tb00919.x.

Stamm, K., & Weis, R. (1980). Patterns of community identification—Their relationship to subscribing, readership and dimensions of news interests. Special Research Report prepared for the ANPA News Research Center.

Stamm, K., & Weis, R. (1982). Toward a dynamic theory of newspaper subscribing. https://doi.org/10.1177/107769908205900304.

Sutton, W., & Kolaja, J. (1960). The concept of community. *Rural Sociology,* 25:197–203.

Taylor, C. (1945). Techniques of community study and analyses as applied to modern civilized society. In Linton, R. (ed.), *The Science of Man in the World Crisis*. Columbia University Press.

Weis, R. (1982). A dynamic view of questioning in an organization. Unpublished doctoral dissertation. Univ. of Washington.

Weis, R. (2003). A generous mentor and advisor, in Dervin, B., & Chaffee, S,. with Foreman-Wernet, L. (eds.). *Communication, A different kind of horse race: Essays honoring Richard F. Carter*. Hampton Press.

Weis, R. (2019a). Speech Doctor No. 30: What Program Chairs Look For. Private email to clients, Weis Communications, Feb. 27.

Weis, R. (2019b). Speech Doctor No. 31: What Program Conference Organizers Look For. Private email to clients, Weis Communications, Mar. 18.

Weis, R. (2019c). Speech Doctor No. 40: Serving on a Panel. Private email to clients, Weis Communications, July 8.

Weis, R. (2019d). Speech Doctor No. 41: Another Perspective on Panels. Private email to clients, Weis Communications, July 15.

Weis, R., & Stamm, K. (1982). The relationship of specific news interests to stages of settling in a community. *Journal of Newspaper Research*.

Weis, R., Stamm, K., Smith, C., Nilan, M., Clark, F., Weis, J., & Kennedy, K. Communities of care and caring: The case of MSWatch.com. *Journal of Health Psychology*, 8:(1) 135–48. https://doi.org/10.1177/1359105303008001449.

Wikipedia (April 28, 2021). https://en.wikipedia.org/wiki/Confucius.

Williams, H. (2019) Pers. communication reprinted with permission, published in Weis, R. (2019c). Speech Doctor No. 41: Another Perspective on Panels. Private email to clients, Weis Communications, July 15.

Young Christian Students Records (YCS), University of Notre Dame Archives (UNDA), Notre Dame, IN 46556. https://archives.nd.edu/findaids/ead/xml/ycs.xml.

Index